Social Work for the Twenty-first Century

Social Work for the Twenty-first Century

Challenges and Opportunities

John T. Pardeck

and

Francis K. O. Yuen

In Memoriam by

Dr. Roland Meinert

 PRAEGER

Westport, Connecticut
London

Library of Congress Cataloging-in-Publication Data

Pardeck, John T.
    Social work for the twenty-first century : challenges and
opportunities / John T. Pardeck and Francis K. O. Yuen.
      p. cm.
    Includes bibliographical references and index.
    ISBN 0–275–97893–1 (alk. paper)
    1. Social work education. 2. Social service–Philosophy.
    3. Social workers–Training of. I. Yuen, Francis K. O. II. Title.
    HV11.P32   2006
    361.3′2–dc22   2005034110

British Library Cataloguing in Publication Data is available.

Library of Congress Catalog Card Number: 2005034110
ISBN: 0–275–97893–1

First published in 2006

Praeger Publishers, 88 Post Road West, Westport, CT 06881
An imprint of Greenwood Publishing Group, Inc.
www.praeger.com

Printed in the United States of America

The paper used in this book complies with the
Permanent Paper Standard issued by the National
Information Standards Organization (Z39.48–1984).

10 9 8 7 6 5 4 3 2

Dedicated to:

Dr. John T. Pardeck

Contents

Preface

In November 2003, Dr. John Terry Pardeck called and asked me to join him on a book project that he had been working on for some time about social work in the century. I had an uneasy feeling about the call. In our prior conversations, he had been very excited about writing and completing this book. He explained that the draft of all the chapters of the book was more than half finished. He needed someone to work with him to finish the rest of the book. Although we had co-authored many publications, I knew that this was a very personal project for him. I was surprised and unsettled by his sudden invitation. Nevertheless, I agreed to join him on this book project. Several months later, Terry called and wanted me to promise him that I would complete this book. He also told me the reason for his request.

Terry had been instrumental in guiding newer faculty members including myself into academic publications and always encouraged faculty to do basic research. He was a true social worker, a scholar, and an educator. He cared most about the vulnerable populations in our society, particularly children and people with disabilities. He never refused to take a stand for the exploited and the oppressed. Terry was a prolific writer who published many books and articles. His areas of expertise also spanned a wide range from disability, children's rights, and social work education, to bibliotherapy. I am honored to complete this book project with Terry, and I have tried to preserve Terry's style and viewpoints wherever possible.

In this book, Terry argued that the future of the social work profession relies on its ability to establish its exclusive knowledge base through scientific inquiries. He summarized the essence of this book.

Examining social work from a historical perspective over the past century reveals that it was an emerging quasi-profession during its first thirty-five years. This was followed by fifty years of growth and development during which it finally achieved greater professional status and wider societal acceptance. However, beginning in the late 1980s there began to appear signs that the level of achievement in both practice and education was leveling off and was not as stable as had been thought. Predictions began to be made that social work practice as it had been known might be at an end, and social work education was characterized as having deep-seated problems. Stultification and petrification were noted in the educational process, and there were calls for widespread innovation during the next millennium. Professional paradigms were being called into question as the profession struggled to retain its earlier identity.

Now even though the number of professionally educated social workers is at an all time high, the specific needs they are to serve and the unique role assigned to them by the larger society have become blurred. Many find it difficult to give a clear answer to the question: "What do social workers do?" Some scholars see the problem in that social work no longer has an overarching theoretical base to organize and guide practitioner behavior. Others willfully seek to deconstruct earlier theoretical anchorages in social work and replace them with the increasingly popular assertions of postmodern philosophy. The postmodern approach also casts aside the earlier marriage to traditional social science, which made relatives of social work and other more established social science professions. Social work lacks an epistemological handbook to help it accommodate to the explosion of technological developments. It also lacks an organizing theory and knowledge base. The challenge of social work in the twenty-first century is to develop a greater appreciation for traditional social science and to work toward a theory and knowledge base unique to the field of social work.

Unfortunately, social work is often perceived as a non-rigorous and anti-intellectual discipline both in the professional and academic communities. Some have recalled the feeling of being the "second best" in these communities: "My cousin did not get into nursing school so she became a social work major!" "Since he could not be a Ph.D. psychologist, he got his MSW instead!" Meanwhile, many social workers are wondering why we need to explain and defend our profession. We do so much for so many but we cannot, with great confidence, tell people precisely and succinctly what we know, what we do, and how well we do it. Authors of this book argue that among the reasons that contribute to this situation are the profession's lack of a solid knowledge base and a commitment to scholarly activities including publication and practice research.

In our efforts to be accountable to our funding sources and our clients, quantitative research helps provide the numbers that satisfy many of the demands for reporting. It also supplies the important markers to gauge and to measure achievement and progress. These numbers, however, can be rather dry. "Thirty out of the 40 clients who received this particular social work intervention for at least two months have attained 80 percent of their stated goals and experienced a significant increase in their abilities to handle similar crises according to their responses on the Ability Inventory." These clients can easily become statistics and their stories of success or failure are often told through the numeric indicators. Qualitative studies help us put the human stories back onto these statistics. Qualitative and quantitative research methodologies have their unique and important places in developing social work knowledge. The profession needs established and validated evidence to show what we know, what has happened, what has changed, and what the impacts are for the intended change. This requires on-going systematic research and dissemination of findings for the development and refinement of the knowledge base for the profession.

Specifically, in this book, Terry argues the following key points:

1. With the rise of postmodern adherents in social work there has been a concomitant effort on other meta-narratives or paradigms as organizing frameworks for professional practice. The postmodern approach to social work practice has drastically altered the ethos of the profession and the manner in which practitioners go about their craft. In order for the profession to continue to grow and become a respectful profession, social work needs to engage in rigorous scientific inquiry to develop its unique knowledge base.
2. The problems that face social work practitioners are evident in the institution of social work education. They manifest themselves in two major areas. The first has epistemological dimensions concerning the manner in which the knowledge, skills, and values for practice are developed and transmitted. The second concerns the process and the dynamics of the accreditation of social work education programs.
3. The field of social work possesses the capacity and has the opportunity to engage in actions to remediate the problems it faces in the twenty-first century. The field of social work needs to generate sufficient collective insight and willingness to take the required actions for change. Improvements are required in many areas; this book focuses on five areas that need immediate attention for change.

This book takes on a critical position to assess the various aspects of social work practice and education. It argues that social work is still a profession searching for a firm identity and a clear and respectful image that social workers and others could identify. The incorporation of science and a scientific approach to social work education and practice appears to be the key for the profession to continue to grow and to gain its rightful place in the professional and academic communities. Lastly, this book is intended to generate productive dialogues to advance the profession and its education processes.

Francis K. O. Yuen, DSW
Professor
Division of Social Work
California State University
Sacramento

In Memoriam

With the recent passing of John Terry Pardeck several of the most vulnerable groups in society lost a dedicated, spirited, and unwavering advocate. These included children, families, the mentally ill, and persons with disabilities. Unlike some advocates who are highly effective in a narrow sphere of activity, Terry operated at many levels as direct practitioner, academic, community leader, policy analyst, and author for professional journals, books, and op-ed pieces in newspapers.

I first met Terry in 1990 when he was a candidate for a faculty position in a social work education program that I chaired. Of those who applied he was clearly the most qualified on the basis of his teaching, research, and community service experience. Several faculty questioned whether he would be a good fit for the program that was very experience- and direct-practice based while Terry's strong points appeared to be in the areas of research and scholarship. Hiring Terry proved to be one of the best personnel decisions of my career. As this program developed Terry continued his scholarly output and served as a role model and mentor to other faculty who later joined the program. As a result of all their work this relatively small program eventually ranked above many programs of greater size in this regard.

By any measurement Terry's scholarly publication record was outstanding and included 25 books and over 130 articles in professional and disciplinary peer-reviewed journals. The scope of his research and writings was broad and embraced such areas as bibliotherapy, family health, homelessness, computers, children's rights, reproductive policy, and many topics in the field of disability. His productivity led to many academic honors and fellowships. He took his ideas beyond the academic setting and applied them to real world issues and policies. In this regard he provided leadership to assist the Missouri Association for Social Welfare to achieve its statewide social justice mission. He also assisted the Missouri Protection and Advocacy organization to advance the civil rights of persons with disabilities by both advocacy and litigation.

After the Americans with Disabilities Act was passed in 1990 Terry became a vigorous advocate on behalf of students with disabilities at Southwest Missouri State University. Along with others he persistently urged that both the Council on Social Work Education and the National Association of Social Work become more sensitive and responsive to persons with disabilities. His belief that main line social journals did not provide adequate coverage of disability issues led to the establishment of the *Journal of Social Work In Disability & Rehabilitation*. He remained editor until the time of his death.

Terry did not shy away from conducting research in areas that were sensitive to the fields of social work education and practice. He was convinced, for example, that many persons appointed to the editorial boards of social work journals did not possess the qualifications to serve as gatekeepers of the information and knowledge being disseminated to practitioners. He maintained that appointments to these boards were being made on the basis of "old boy" and "old girl" relationships and not on the basis of merit and achievement on the part of reviewers. His research documented that social work editorial boards lacked achievement in publications and they were far below the achievement of editorial boards in related fields.

In the classroom Terry brought a high degree of rigorous preparation and mastery to the subject matter at hand. He set high standards for students and consistently received glowing student course evaluations. In an age when many graduate level courses are merely wide ranging group discussions Terry presented substantive content. He also believed that professors must "profess" and he articulated for students a set of values to be carried over into professional practice.

When faced with the option of acceptance by peers as opposed to the search for truth Terry always opted for the latter. Along the way he ruffled a few professional feathers that needed to be ruffled, but it was always to seek out the path to benefit those most in need. When the attributes of professionalism such as altruism, integrity, objectivity, and quest for truth are considered it is obvious that Terry possessed them to a high degree.

Early in his career Terry fought gallantly against a debilitating disease. He later enjoyed years of remission until the last few years when he again became seriously ill. Although in recent years there was geographic distance between us Terry and I communicated electronically about writing and other projects. He never once complained about his illness and until the final days of his life continued with his love of writing. He left a body of substantive work that contributed to the advancement of his chosen profession. Terry left us at the height of his professional and intellectual capacity and the loss to his wife and sons, the profession of social work, and his many colleagues is profound.

Roland Meinert, Ph.D.
Former Director of schools of social work at Michigan State University,
the University of Missouri and Southwest Missouri State University
Past President, Missouri Association for Social Welfare
Past Chair, Missouri Protection and Advocacy, Inc.

Chapter 1

Introduction

Moving into the twenty-first century, the field of social work is a little over one hundred years old. Whether social work has reached full professional status is still a topic that generates many debates. The answer to this question probably depends on the model used to determine if an occupation meets the model's criteria for professional status.

In the early developmental stages of social work, there was an important debate between those who viewed social work as a profession aimed at bringing about institutional changes versus those who argued social work should focus on change at the individual level. Popple and Leighniner (2004) report that Edith Abbot, George Mangold, and Samuel McCune Lindsey were all early advocates of the institutional change focus to social work. This group felt it was important to work for social reform at the legislative level as well as other macro kinds of intervention. Frank Burno and Mary Richmond, however, strongly advocated for a professional approach to social work practice focusing on changing individuals and not necessarily social institutions. Even though there was this disagreement between the two groups concerning practice orientation, most social workers during this early period felt they were part of a profession.

In 1915, Abraham Flexner presented a paper at the National Conference of Charities and Corrections that challenged the notion that social work had achieved professional status. Flexner made it clear in his presentation to the conference attendants that social work was not a profession as defined by his model outlining professional status (Meinert, Pardeck, and Kreuger, 2000). Under Flexner's model, the following components had to be present to achieve professional status:

1. Intellectual operation with large individual responsibility.
2. A knowledge base drawn from science and learning.
3. Possession of an educationally communicable technique.
4. Self-organization.

Flexner concluded that social work possessed some of the above components, but not all. The area he found particularly lacking was a clear educationally communicable technique. This problem continues to plague social work today. Social work does not have a clear educationally communicable technique because it lacks a solid knowledge base; it has not effectively integrated the basic canons of social science for knowledge development; and suffers from a low social status within the University setting because of its commitment to, among other issues, the promotion of ideology and not academic rigor (Meinert, Pardeck, and Kreuger, 2000). A leading academic in the field of social work, Duncan Lindsey, captures this sentiment through the quote below:

The few cases I have illustrated here are being repeated many times over through the profession. Although I believe they are due largely to a kind of hidebound, inflexible habit or traditionalism that has failed to recognize the imperatives facing the profession muttering, of cronyism and favoritism are now being heard from many corners. My concern is that many talented and gifted researchers have grown disillusioned, with some so disillusioned they are ready to abandon the entire field as unsalvageable. Certainly, until we are resolute in upholding research standards, we will be failing our clients and in danger of failing as a profession as well (1999, p. 119).

SOCIAL WORK KNOWLEDGE

Many social science professions and disciplines have established clear logics for the development of their knowledge base. These logics are often grounded in science. Science obtains objective knowledge through systematic data collection and analysis methodologies that are logical, observable, repeatable, and objective. Logical and scientific knowledge, however, is only one of the sources for knowledge development. Atherton and Klemmack (1982) and Yuen (1999) discuss the four main sources of knowledge. They include tradition, experience, common sense, and scientific knowledge.

Tradition provides a type of knowledge and practice that is based on custom, repetition, and habit. It is often found in ancient wisdom and is used as a guide for understanding the world. "Tradition is customs and beliefs that have been handed down from generation to generation. It is not necessarily logical or rational, but it makes sense to people who practice it" (Yuen, 1999, p. 106). This type of belief has somehow been developed in the past, held by the current generation, and continues to evolve. Having chicken soup when one has a cold is such a traditional belief. At times, traditions are false and biased beliefs or practices that have passed on to the current population. Some parents still believe in the use of corporal punishment for disciplining children, while others have particular negative or unfounded perceptions about persons with disabilities or persons of a particular cultural group. Unfortunately, some of these false beliefs reinforce prejudice and discrimination. Obviously, it is unlikely a social worker will endorse traditional beliefs concerning the importance of corporal punishment for correcting children's behavior or those that reinforce discrimination against oppressed groups such as persons with disabilities.

One example of this kind of tradition, appearing in some social work curricula, is the emphasis on psychodynamic models that are used commonly in clinical practice. Although the efficacy of the psychodynamic models have been questioned, they continue to be part of the social work tradition and be included in social work curricula along with other more tested practice models. For example, Brian (1990) asserts that what is known to work effectively for changing individual behavior is the cognitive-behavior approaches. Reid (Reid and Epstein, 1972; Reid, 1978; 1992; Epstein 1992) champions the use of task-centered approaches. Thyer (1997) suggests that not including models of intervention that have been proven to work in the social work curricula is simply unethical on the part of the social work faculty.

Social work faculty and practitioners heavily endorse knowledge that is based on their personal or professional experience. The Council on Social Work Education (CSWE), the accreditation body for social work programs within the United States, has accreditation guidelines for undergraduate and graduate programs which require that anyone teaching a practice class must have at least two years of post-Master of Social Work (MSW) practice experience. It is undeniable that rich practice experiences of the instructors increase the likelihood of the relevancy of the teaching. Paradoxically, a doctoral degree in social work is not called for to teach practice courses. What thus appears to be emphasized is experience, and in some cases just two years of experience, over the supposedly rigorous doctoral academic requirements. Certainly, a doctorate level faculty with an MSW and years of practice experience is preferred by many programs and students to teach practice classes.

The Group for the Advancement of Doctoral Education (GADE) (2003) uses three independent and interrelated concepts to define social work and to assert the purpose of doctoral education in social work. Social work can be distinguished as: (1) a *practical activity*, reflected in its publicly visible role as a "helping profession" with a commitment to developing and using practical methods of support, intervention, and change in a variety of contexts, particularly those pertaining to disadvantaged and vulnerable population; (2) a *discipline*, reflected in an emphasis on establishing and maintaining social work as a subject worthy of scientific study and development in its own right within the framework of higher education; and (3) a *research tradition*, reflected in an emphasis on building a particular body of theoretical, empirical, and applied knowledge, as well as infrastructure for its support, adjudication and dissemination (Tucker, 2002). The province of doctoral education in social work is primarily with social work as discipline and research tradition. Hence, its main purpose is to prepare social work scholars and researchers of the highest quality so that they may make significant contributions to social work education as well as to the scientific and professional literature in social work and social welfare (retrieved from <http://web.uconn.edu/gade/gadeguidelines.pdf> on 12/26/2005).

Doctoral social work programs in general place a heavier emphasis on social scientific theories and research methodologies. While the MSW is considered a terminal degree to prepare its students for practice, a doctoral degree in social work would prepare students to engage in research and teaching. For the last 20 years, the change in the degree offered, from Doctor of Social Work (DSW), a professional degree, to Doctor of Philosophy (Ph.D.), reflects social work schools' increased emphasis on research among doctoral level social workers. While it is reasonable to require sufficient practice experience for instructors who teach practice courses, one has to question the rationale behind requiring minimum practice experience over academic credentials. What is interesting about the CSWE requirement of two years of practice experience before one can teach a practice course in the social work curriculum? There is also no mention of the quality or kind of practice experience one must have.

Experience as a source of knowledge often forms the base of our inductive learning (Bein, Yuen, and Lum, 2003). It should however be used with great caution because it has a number of serious limitations (Pardeck and Yuen, 2001). One important limitation is that human perception is extremely unreliable. Perception is shaped, among other things, by one's culture, socialization, and personal bias. Specifically, human beings construct their own realities through experience, and often these realities are very different between individuals and groups.

Another limitation of knowledge based on experience is that this kind of knowledge does not result from direct perception but rather from inferences made about those perceptions (Pardeck and Yuen, 2001). Experience is subjective. It lacks the ability to generalize and infer. One person's bad experience with family therapy is not sufficient to support the claim that family therapy is not effective for all people.

Experience is also affected by special interests. For example, some social workers may, for whatever reasons, have a vested interest in finding that a certain treatment approach is effective and they will find accordingly. Another limitation of experiential knowledge is that the sample of experiences one has had only represents a very narrow population of people and may simply not be indicative of larger populations.

When knowledge is built on tradition and experience it often blends into what is referred to as common sense (Yuen, 1999). Common sense knowledge is contextual. Common sense for people with a particular background is not necessarily a shared common sense for another group. It is common sense for Americans to know a big dinner with turkey is often prepared to celebrate Thanksgiving. It is however not at all common sense for a group of new immigrants from Laos. It is common sense for local residents not to go to a particular area of town after dark because it is a well-known high-crime area; but an out-of-town visitor may not be aware of that concern at all. Common sense is grounded in tradition, experience, wisdom, and, sometimes, prejudice.

Common sense knowledge does not involve rigorous and systematic approaches to distinguishing fact from fiction. As a basis for social work practice, knowledge needs to be based on rigor and systematic methods; common sense or a vague feeling that a practitioner is helping a client is not enough (Pardeck and Yuen, 2001).

In spite of their limitations, tradition, experience, and common sense form the basic worldview for people and they are also the operating framework for social workers. The traditions and experiences of the professional, the clients, the community, and the great social environment provide the contexts for social work practice to take place. Experience is important. It is difficult to learn how to ride a bike by only reading a "how to" book. It takes trials and errors, skinned knees, disappointments, a bruised ego, and eventually successful attempts to master the skill. It is about learning and practicing.

Social work is a practice profession and thus, practice experience is absolutely essential. It is with the tradition of social work, that is, respect for human diversity, advocacy for social justice, and the accumulated practice-wisdom that social workers could develop the "professional common sense" (Yuen, 1999). It is a condition that has been integrated into their well-developed skills and knowledge, which are put to use as if they are their second nature.

Having tradition, experience, and professional common sense is not enough. A very helpful older lady who lives down the street has more tradition, experience, and common sense than most of the recent social work graduates from a local university. She is a very kind and wise lady whom the neighbors love and respect. She is however not a professional social worker. She is a very helpful person who has a lot to offer. She is operating out of her subjective and personal knowledge, that is, tradition, experience, and common sense. Professional social work education, supposedly, provides the avenues to learn and to develop scientifically developed knowledge and skills for effective and professional social work practice.

When science is used as the approach for generating knowledge, one uses systematic ways to collect and analyze data and to present the results. Science has distinguishing characteristics. It is empirical, systematic, attempts to identify cause, findings are provisional, and lastly, objectivity is a necessity to minimize bias.

Empirical approaches employ scientific methods that are based on experimental methods, direct observation, and other systematic ways to learn and understand the social world. Findings concerning social phenomena are always provisional because one continues to question and refute what may be presently known about a phenomenon. Finally, one who uses science as a source of knowledge attempts to be objective by removing personal or participants' biases when reaching conclusions about the social or physical world. One of the important issues facing social work in the twenty-first century will be deciding on the strategies to build social work knowledge. That is, will social work knowledge be developed from systematic approaches endorsed by science and evidences? Or, will the field of social work build knowledge on postmodern interpretations of the social world? The method used may well determine if social work survives as a field of study in the university setting.

SOCIAL SCIENCE THEORY AND SOCIAL WORK

The ecological perspective and systems theory have been dominant theories in the field of social work. Both theories are borrowed from other academic disciplines and have been interpreted by social work writers as useful perspectives for assessing and treating client problems at both the micro and macro levels. The work of Germain (1973) and Hartman (1970) amplifies the field's unique understanding of ecological and systems theories. They both stress that each theory helps practitioners in their assessment and treatment of client problems. Both suggest that ecological and systems theories offer useful frameworks for conducting practice at all levels of intervention.

The ecological perspective is based on the metaphor of biological organisms that live and adapt in complex networks of environmental forces. It is grounded in an evolutionary, adaptive view of human beings in continuous transaction and interaction with their physical and social environment. According to ecological theory, both the person and the environment continuously change and accommodate one another. Ecological perspective stresses that people and environments are holistic and transactional. The following comprise a number of important terms and concepts stressed in ecological perspective (Meinert, Pardeck, and Kreuger, 2000):

1. Transactions are understood as continuous reciprocal exchanges in the person–environment system. Through these exchanges, each shapes, changes, or otherwise influences the other over time.
2. The concept of life stress refers to either a positive or a negative person–environment relationship.
3. The concept of coping to the special adaptations that are made in response to internal stress.
4. Habitat refers to the place where a person or family lives.
5. A niche is perceived as the result of one's accommodation to the environment.
6. The concept of relatedness, based on attachment theory, incorporates ideas about emotional and social loneliness and isolation.

A variety of practice roles and models are called for in employing ecological perspectives in social work practice, including advocacy, policy and planning, primary prevention, and research. Furthermore, the practitioner must understand how human growth and development, and social functioning take place in the context of ecological systems. This is obviously an extremely complex process involving numerous variables. The practitioner must have knowledge of diverse systems at the micro, mezzo, and macro levels.

Systems theory is a theoretical underpinning of the ecological approach to practice. The aim of systems theory is to help the practitioner understand how the client system is influenced by and affects the greater social ecology. It is critical of a reductionistic view of human behavior and stresses behavior can best be understood in the context of the various social systems such as the family system. Assumptions guiding a systems theory approach to practice include the following (Meinert, Pardeck, and Kreuger, 2000):

1. Wholeness suggests change in one part of a system causes changes throughout the system.
2. Feedback regulates a system through inputs.
3. Equifinality suggests there is more than one way to get to a final state.
4. Circular causality is used to understand system functioning. Systems theory does not endorse linear thinking as a means for understanding human behavior.

Ecological perspective and systems theory provide useful frameworks that help social workers in assessment and planning for intervention. Although they are heavily stressed in social work programs throughout the United States, they also have many limitations. Among the limitations is that they are not empirically tested theories. One can even argue that they are no more than ideologies passing as social scientific theory. Application of ecological and systems theories to social work practice would have to have the following considerations:

1. The client system must adapt to the environment; this kind of adaptation may be viewed as oppressive.
2. Each theory involves numerous variables for understanding human behavior and social functioning. This complexity is difficult to translate into effective practice.
3. Systems subordinate individuals, families, creativity, and autonomy.
4. Little or no scientific validation has been offered supporting the theories.

These assessments are echoed by many including Brueggemann (2002) who comments that ecological and systems theories view people as "atomistic rather than as social beings" (p. 20). People are like parts of a machine such that "Humans are not seen as actors who decide for themselves, but are only capable of adapting in response to changes in their social environment" (p. 20).

Ecological perspectives and systems theory do indeed offer a comprehensive perspective for guiding social work intervention at multiple levels, even though they lack social scientific validation. The CSWE accreditation guidelines emphasize that both theories need to be stressed in the social work curriculum (1994). Thyer (1997) notes that social work has a tradition of relying more on ideology than social science as a guide to practice.

POSITIVISM VERSUS POSTMODERNISM

Hartman (1990) in an editorial in the journal *Social Work* concluded that "both the scientific and the artistic methods provide us with ways of knowing" (p. 4). She pointed out that "there are indeed many ways of knowing and many kinds of knowers: researchers, practitioners, clients. Some seekers of truth may take a path that demands distance and objectivity, whereas others rely on deeply personal and empathic knowing" (p. 4).

Meinert, Pardeck, and Kreuger (2000), however, argued in their work that the field of social work is heavily grounded in the postmodern epistemology. Postmodernism as an alternative paradigm to positivism is associated with perspectives that include relativism, linguistic philosophy, and constructivism (Gellner, 1992). Meinert, Pardeck, and Kreuger (2000) believe that this tradition has resulted in a weak knowledge and theoretical base that seems to be interpreted and re-interpreted by each new generation of social workers. It should be noted that the CSWE has traditionally endorsed models of knowledge development based on positivism. Yet the attitude of social workers who graduate from accredited programs appears to be one that is anti-positivistic. At the same time, social workers often endorse knowledge development based on ideology and experience that are grounded more in the postmodern tradition than positivism. Positivism and postmodernism offer uniquely different worldviews for understanding social reality.

Positivism has been a dominant epistemology in Western culture since the nineteenth century. Meinert, Pardeck, and Kreuger (2000) summarize the basic tenets of positivism: 1. Reality exists independent of the individual. 2. Absolute truth can be discovered. 3. Knowledge consists of verifiable facts that exist independent of the person. 4. Meaning is external to symbols. 5. Understanding and knowing results from categorizing concepts. 6. Science is the core methodology for discovering truth. 7. Causality can be discovered through the scientific method. 8. Individual behavior is determinant.

Postmodernism presents a much different view of the social world. Meinert, Pardeck, and Kreuger (2000) discuss some of the more important tenets of postmodernism: 1. Reality is constructed by the individual or group. 2. Truths are relative to time and place and constructed by individuals and groups. 3. Knowledge is nothing more than a social construct. 4. Meaning and understanding emerge from social interaction. 5. Knowing is an ongoing process of interpretation of events by individuals and groups. 6. Science is an interpretative process unique to the individual and group making the observation. 7. Causality is a complex process involving numerous elements and events. 8. Behavior of individuals is indeterminate.

Positivism advocates that reality is independent of the individual; postmodernism suggests the individual and group socially construct reality. Truth is relative to the individual and group according to the postmodern perspective; whereas a positivist tradition concludes truth can be seen as an absolute. Knowledge development from a positivist approach results from the categorizing of concepts; the postmodern approach concludes that knowledge is fluid and changes through time with the individual and group. The postmodernist views science as a process unique to the individual observer; the positivist uses science as the core methodology of discovering knowledge.

A postmodern approach to knowledge development appears to be chaotic because individuals and groups are viewed as systems that continually re-invent it. What is understood as knowledge one day is negated the next by persons or groups. This process would appear to result in a lack of clear knowledge boundaries for the field or discipline that endorses a postmodern perspective. On the other hand, it does highlight the power of words and meaning that could shape people's lives. This book will argue that if social work wants to become a respectable field of study and practice, it must put more emphasis on methodologies that incorporate elements of positivism with a clear acknowledgment of its obvious limitations. Alternative paradigms such as postmodernism have many practice advantages and their methodologies should be included. However, their utilities as the most effective means to advance the development of the social work profession remain unclear.

SOCIAL WORK EDITORS AND EDITORIAL BOARDS

Refereed journals are critical to the development of knowledge within professions and academic disciplines. The editors and editorial board members of journals play a critical part in determining what articles are to be published in a field or discipline. Since the 1970s a number of researchers have explored the scholarly productivity of social work editorial boards. These studies have generally found that members of editorial boards of most social work journals fall short in the area of scholarly productivity. A recent study of the publication records of journal editors by Pardeck (2002) provides preliminary findings that this may also be the case for social work editors as well. Given the findings one would have to question the quality and the fairness of the selection of articles published in the field's journals.

Lindsey (1976, 1977) was among the first scholars to conduct research on the scholarly productivity of social work editorial boards. Lindsey reported that social work editorial board members typically lacked distinction and achievement in the area of scholarly productivity. Pardeck (1992a,b) replicated much of Lindsey's research almost two decades later and found the same results again.

Pardeck and Meinert (1999) argued in another study on editorial boards that the field might be less than honest about the quality of social work editorial boards. They found that one of the leading journals in the field, *Social Work*, claimed that members of its editorial board were experts in their areas of specialization and had strong records of scholarly productivity. Pardeck and Meinert found, however, that half of the editorial board of *Social Work* from 1990 to 1995 had not published an article and were cited only three times or less by other scholars. The consulting editors for *Social Work* had similar records of scholarly productivity. For example, 19 percent had not published during the time period studied. The findings by Pardeck and Meinert clearly question the credibility of one of the most important journals in the field.

Epstein (1992) in his research on social work editorial boards found that reviewers of manuscripts submitted for publication were frequently inaccurate, incoherent, and lacked an understanding of basic research methodology. Epstein concluded that his research findings were simply another example of the poor intellectual climate in the field of social work.

Lindsey (1999), in a more recent argument on the poor quality of social work editorial boards, argued that these boards often use nonscientific and idiosyncratic standards for making decisions about the quality of articles submitted for publication. Furthermore, he suggested that the same kind of standards might also be employed by schools of social work when they select faculty for professorships. He found that a number of major research universities with endowed professorships appointed individuals to these positions based on criteria that did not appear to include scholarship. For example, one individual was appointed to an endowed chair at a major research university without one significant publication to the person's credit. Another major university with an endowed chair in social work appointed an individual, to a professorship, who had never been cited in the literature. As Lindsey correctly concludes, no other related discipline to social work such as psychology or sociology would endorse this kind of appointment to an endowed professorship at a major research institution. It will be argued in this book that this type of lack in scholarship may result in the lack of prestige of social work programs among academics.

The status of social work within the university community and for that matter among other professions will increase only if the field attempts to endorse approaches to knowledge development grounded in the traditional scientific tenets found with the social sciences. Furthermore, as long as the field of social work appoints individuals to editorial boards lacking scholarly distinction and uses criteria other than scholarship for professorship appointments, the prestige of social work within and outside the academic field will continue to suffer.

REFERENCES

Atherton, C. & Klemmack, D. (1982). *Research methods in social work*. Lexington, MA: D.C. Heath.

Bein, A., Yuen, F., & Lum, D. (2003). Inductive learning. In D. Lum (Ed.), *Culturally competent practice: A framework for understanding diverse groups and justice issues* (2nd ed.), pp. 165–194. Pacific Grove, CA: Brooks/Cole.

Brian, S. (1990). Empiricism and clinical practice. In L. Videka-Sherman & W. J. Reid (Eds.), *Advances in clinical social work research* (pp. 1–7). Silver Springs, MD: National Association of Social Workers.

Brueggemann, W. G. (2002). *The practice of macro social work* (2nd ed.). Belmont, CA: Brooks/Cole.

Commission on accreditation (1994). *Handbook of accreditation standards and procedures*. Washington, DC: Council on social work education.

Epstein, W. M. (1992). A response to Pardeck. Thump therapy for social work journals. *Research on Social Work Practice, 2*, 525–528.

Gellner, E. (1992). *Postmodernism, reason and religion*. London: Routledge.

Germain, C. (1973). An ecological perspective in casework. *Social Casework, 54*, 323–330.

Group for the Advancement of Doctoral Education (2003). *Guidelines for Quality in Social Work Doctoral Programs (Revised) 2003*. Retrieved December 26, 2005 from <http://web.uconn.edu/gade/gadeguidelines.pdf>.

Hartman, A. (1970). To think about the unthinkable. *Social Casework, 50*, 467–474.

Hartman, A. (January 1990). Many ways of knowing (Editorial). *Social Work*, (35)1, 3–4.

Lindsey, D. (1976). Distinction, achievement, and editorial board membership. *American Psychologist*, 31, 799–804.

Lindsey, D. (1977). Participation and influence in publication review proceedings: A reply. *American Psychologist*, 32(7), 579–586.

Lindsey, D. (1999). Ensuring standards in social work research. *Research on Social Work Practice*, 9, 115–120.

Meinert, R., Pardeck, J. T., & Kreuger, L. (2000). *Social work: Seeking relevancy in the twenty-first century*. Binghamton, NY: The Haworth Press.

Pardeck, J. T. (1992a). Are social work editorial boards competent: Some disquieting data with implications for social work practice. *Research on Social Work Practice*, 2(4), 487–496.

Pardeck, J. T. (1992b). The distinction and achievement levels of social work editorial boards revisited. *Research on Social Work Practice*, 2(4), 529–537.

Pardeck, J. T. & Meinert, R. (1999). Scholarly achievements of the social work editorial board and consulting editors: A commentary. *Research on Social Work Practice*, 9, 86–91.

Pardeck, J. T. & Yuen, F. K. O. (Eds.) (1999). *Family health: A holistic approach to social work practice*. Westport, CT: Auburn House.

Pardeck, J. & Yuen, F. K. O. (2001). Family health: An emerging paradigm for social workers. *Journal of Health and Social Policy*, 13(3), 59–74.

Popple, P. R. & Leighniner, L. (2004). *Policy-based profession: An introduction to social welfare policy analysis for social workers* (3rd ed.). Boston, MA: Allyn and Bacon.

Reid, W. (1978). *The task-centered system*. NY: Columbia University Press.

Reid, W. (1992). *Task strategies: An empirical approach to clinical social work*. NY: Columbia University Press.

Reid, W. & Epstein, L. (1972). *Task-centered casework*. NY: Columbia University Press.

Thyer, B. A. (1997). Effective psychosocial treatments for children: A selective review. In J. T. Pardeck & M. Markward (Eds.), *Reassessing social work practice with children* (pp. 79–89). NY: Gordon and Breach.

Tucker, D. J. (2002). *The Future of Doctoral Social Work Education. The Future We Would Like vs. its Likely Future*. Paper presented as part of a panel on The Future of Education in Doctoral Social Work, Annual Program Meeting of the Council for Social Work Education.

Yuen, F. K. O. (1999). Family Health and Cultural Diversity. In J. T. Pardeck & F. K. O. Yuen (Eds.), *Family health: A holistic approach to social work practice* (pp. 101–113). Westport, CT: Auburn House.

Chapter 2

Diverse Social Work Practices

I n this chapter, the common methods used in social work practices are discussed. Several more empirically grounded clinical approaches including the ecosystem-oriented intervention proposed by one of the authors, Pardeck (1996), will be discussed. Finally, various clinical instruments that could further improve social work practices are recommended.

SOCIAL WORK METHODS OF INTERVENTION

The traditional approaches to categorize social work practices with separated interventions (casework, group work, and community organization) are now dated in present day social work practice. Social work practitioners are often called upon to use all three traditional methods and their various intervention skills in an integrated fashion.

Theories and practice have a reciprocal relationship in the development of the social work profession. Payne (1997) provides a detailed and comprehensive analysis of theories that are used in social work and their implications for social work practice and development. Payne's analysis also supplies a framework for many of the discussions in this chapter.

Reid (2002) reviews the trends of knowledge for direct social work practice. He asserts that during the post-World War II period psychoanalytic methods dominated social work practice. Alternative approaches such as "family systems, behavioral, transactional, gestalt, existential, reality, and cognitive" (p. 8) emerged in the 1950s and 1960s. In the 1970s, many more new models including "the generalist, ecosystems, ecological perspective, strengths perspective, feminist practice, empowerment, task-centered, psychoeducational, solution-focused, multicultural, narrative, family preservation, and empirical practice movements" (p. 8) were proposed. Social work as a profession has been opened to these diverse new ideas and practice. Increasingly more practice approaches have applied and integrated different theoretical frameworks and intervention skills into cohesive frameworks for practice. Reid (2002) further cites that many social work educators have observed and described this trend of integration as "personal practice model" (Edward J. Mullen, 1983), "grab bag" (Howard Goldstein, 1990), or "enrichment" (Francis Turner, 1996) approach.

Working with Individuals

There are many models of social work practice with individuals. Looking back into history, social work practitioners working at the individual level of intervention have at various degrees been influenced by the psychodynamic approach to treatment. The psychodynamic approach (Hamilton, 1950; Richmond, 1917), an early social work practice approach, focuses on personality, pathology, and the clients' insight. It is influenced by Sigmund Freud's psychoanalytic approach.

Sigmund Freud (1856–1939) developed psychoanalysis as a therapeutic technique to treat his patients in resolving issues that he believed were repressed in the unconscious. As a body of knowledge and a theory, Freud devised the psychoanalytic theory that consists of models of personality, the conscious (Ego) and unconscious (Id and Super-Ego) mind, psychosexual stages of development, defense mechanisms, and the drive, which is an internal motivation.

The psychodynamic approaches and perspectives are adaptations of the psychoanalytic theory in therapy and hold the view that personality is affected by interactive psychological forces. Well-known theorists who represent the psychodynamic approaches include Carl Jung (1875–1961), Alfred Alder (1870–1937), and Erik Erikson (1902–1994). Since the founding of Freudianism, a great deal has been written about the psychodynamic approach to treatment. Even though many of the ideas associated with this approach have been challenged and criticized as lacking scientific evidence, psychodynamic approaches have heavily influenced modern day clinical social work practice.

Since 1964, Woods and Hollis' psychosocial approach (1990) has incorporated psychodynamic theory with a then new emphasis on "person-in-situation." Through a diagnostic understanding, social worker and client identify problem areas and their relevant personality characteristics. Combining the client's internal strength and the resources in the environment, together they determine appropriate treatment objectives that guide their choice of treatment procedures. The treatment process aims to increase the available opportunity and to improve both the client's personal and interpersonal functioning.

Perlman's (1957) problem-solving social casework approach examines the "4 Ps": person, problem, place, and process. "The person with whom work is done, the problem presented, the place where work is done, and the work process... The focus is how one's ego manages outside relationship" (Payne, 1997, p. 87). Both the client's problems and the difficulties in the environment are to be addressed at the same time. Clients need assistance in increasing their coping capacity and overcoming barriers to solve problems. Perlman's problem-solving social casework leads the way for other problem-solving social work approaches including the crisis intervention approach and the task-centered approach. Her problem-solving approach, however, is less concerned about tasks accomplished and more "concerned with seeing human life as a process of resolving life issues" (Payne, 1997, p. 119).

Based on psychodynamic ego psychology, crisis intervention (Caplan, 1965; Lindemann, 1944, Robert, 1991) focuses on people's emotional responses to crises. Through establishing rapport and appropriate communication, the social worker first attends to the client's safety and feeling, identifies major problems, and considers possible alternatives. Together they develop an action plan with practical tasks that would assist the client to readjust and interrupt events that disrupt normal functioning.

The task-centered approach (Reid and Epstein, 1972; Reid, 1978; 1992; Epstein, 1992) is an integrative and eclectic approach that is not based on any particular psychological or sociological theories. It focuses on practical tasks that improve people's capacities to deal with life's difficulties in a pragmatic manner with defined goals, tasks, and time limits. The social worker's role is to help clients resolve problems and develop the capacity to solve future problems and to seek proper assistance. This approach does not concern much of the underlying causes of people's problems. It does however concern client acceptance of the existence of a problem that can be clearly defined and be resolved through actions. It emphasizes people's abilities and performance in exposing and addressing their own problems.

Case management has been a major professional function for social workers and it continues to evolve as an important practice model.

Case management attempts to assist clients to receive the most appropriate services in a coordinated and timely manner to bring about a desirable change. Rothman and Sager (1998) propose an empirically based "comprehensive psychological enhancement" approach as a new social work practice paradigm for an integrated case management practice with vulnerable populations. Walsh (2000) discusses different case management approaches and functions in mental health. Case management services can range from basic skills training for preventing relapse to proactive skills development for independent living, and strength-based brokering of services to promote the client's success. Walsh suggests that social work case managers who know intimately about the clients' concerns and needs are afforded a unique opportunity for professional intervention. They could play a more direct and therapeutic role in promoting change. Walsh supports the application of a clinical approach of case management that requires the worker to engage in psychotherapeutic intervention, brokering of service, crisis intervention, and consultation.

Working with the Family

The family has always been a key component and a focus for social work practice models. "Social work practice originated in efforts to strengthen and rehabilitate troubled and destitute families" (Laird and Allen, 1983, p. 176). Germain (1983) states "work(ing) with the family unit is as old as social work itself" (p. 27). Traditional social work practice models have always had both the individuals and their environments, most notably families, in mind. Constable and Lee (2004) note "social workers work on both the inside and the outside of families. Their work encompasses family therapy: that is, intervention aimed at restructuring family (and thus personal) patterns from the inside" (p. 4).

Yuen (2005, p. 1) describes a definition of family and its various dimensions.

Family is defined as a system of two or more interacting persons who are either related by ties of marriage, birth, or adoption, or who have chosen to commit themselves in unity for the common purpose of promoting the physical, mental, emotional, social, economic, cultural and spiritual growth and development of the unit and each to its members (Pardeck and Yuen 1999). Family can be further conceptualized by its interrelated dimensions of nature, structure, and function (Pardeck and Yuen 1999; Pardeck et al., 1998).

The rise of the family therapy movement as an interdisciplinary approach to working with clients and their families has influenced many aspects of the practice of social work. Family therapy involves members of a family as the key unit of intervention in the treatment process. Different forms of family therapies may draw from a wide range of theories, including psychodynamic and behavioral approaches. Fundamentally, most of them are influenced by the family systems theory. The emphasis on systems theory has revolutionized how individual pathology is assessed and treated. Systems perspective moves individual pathology from the individual to the family and other systems levels. Family members are interdependent upon each other. Their interrelatedness also helps to differentiate among each other. The family is the starting place for the development of meaning, a sense of self, and a sense of others. It is the source for change and the reserve for power to sustain change.

The family performs and prescribes certain family functions such as rules, roles, communication, proximity, boundary, and hierarchy. There are situations, however, where families fail to perform their functions or meet the needs of the family members. Family therapy as a short-term psychotherapeutic intervention is often used to resolve specific problems within the context of a family or to restore particular family functions. Increasingly, social workers in clinical practice employ brief therapies that incorporate many of the family therapeutic approaches.

There are many approaches to conduct a brief family therapy that sees the family as the core unit and context for intervention. These therapeutic processes focus on the interactions within the family context as the sources, motivations, and goals for change. The following are a few of the more commonly used approaches (Snyder and Ooms, 1992; Franklin and Jordan, 1999).

Structural/Strategic Family Therapy. Jay Haley, a linguist, Don Jackson (1920–1968), a psychiatrist, along with Virginia Satir (1916–1988), a social worker, were with the Mental Research Institute in Palo Alto, CA studying the power, control, rules, and communication within family systems. Haley later joined psychiatrist Salvador Minuchin at the Philadelphia Child Guidance Center to develop Structural Family Therapy. This approach focuses on the here-and-now and employs simple and direct approaches to work with the family. Therapy aims to organize the family into a more functional unit to deal with its authority, boundary, organization, structural issues, and communication problems. The therapist is active and directive. Interventions attempt to change family members' perspectives as well as the family's structure and boundaries to identify alternatives to problems and solutions. Change strategies include reframing, joining the family through various directive and sometimes paradoxical techniques to transform and modify the family structure.

Intergenerational Family Therapy. Psychiatrist Murray Bowen (1913–1990) finds many families are emotionally "stuck together" and family members are not able to differentiate among themselves. The therapist functions as a coach to facilitate behavioral changes. Through the recognition of intergenerational unresolved family issues, family interaction patterns, and knowledge of the family legacy, the therapist assists the individual family member to become unstuck and to develop differentiation among family individuals. The construction of a Genogram is commonly used to facilitate the process.

Experiential and Communications Family Therapy. Carl Whitaker, a psychiatrist, focuses on creativity and intuition. He pioneered the experiential approach to psychotherapy in the 1950s. Relying less on theory and techniques, Whitaker works with family members individually one at a time and then collectively to assist the family to develop its own theory of living. It is through increased awareness and sense of choice along with the therapist's support that a therapeutic change is evolved. Virginia Satir develops Communications Therapy that employs creative and experiential activities such as family sculpting to address dysfunctioning in the family. She believes low self-esteem, reinforced by the family members, is often the major contributing factor for the dysfunctions.

Behavioral and Cognitive-Behavioral Family Therapy. Behavioral theory (Skinner, 1974), social learning theory (Bandura, 1977), and cognitive theory (Beck, 1989; Ellis, 1962) are the basic theoretical frameworks for this category of family therapy. Many specific interventions and models such as Functional Family Therapy, Integrative Family Therapy, and Rational-Emotive Therapy (Rational-Emotive Behavioral Therapy) are clustered under this category. It is an eclectic collection of individual treatment models that have been applied to couples and families. Therapeutic approaches in this category place more emphasis on the use of scientific and rational methods to conduct assessment, intervention, and evaluation. Behavioral contracting, thought stopping, anger controlling, and aversive consequences are some of the intervention techniques. Behavioral and Cognitive-Behavioral approaches also inform programs such as parent training, family psycho-education, and family preservation.

Solution-Focused Brief Family Therapy. Social workers Steve de Shazer and Insoo Kim Berg developed the original Solution Focused Therapy. It is a strengths-based therapy model that stresses respect for clients' capacities to solve their own problems and charges the therapist with creating a context in which this can happen (Franklin and Jordan, 1999). Solution-focused therapy is a time-limited, goal-oriented, and behavioral-directed approach. It focuses on working with clients to develop new behaviors that can lead them to the solution of their problems. At the therapy session, a therapist will use sequences that include a miracle question, a scaling question, and compliments or homework. Franklin and Jordan (1999) report Kral's (1995) 5 Ds of Solution Focused Therapy- "develop an image of a realistic solution...discover how and in what ways... determine small, measurable steps (goals)...describe those thoughts, actions, feeling that can help obtain the goals... and do something to make a difference" (p. 111).

Narrative Family Practice. Narrative family therapy is a postmodern therapy that views problems as stories that people tell themselves. It is the clients' view of what is problematic to them. Although the amount of direction by therapists varies, the narrative therapist listens to client-generated stories, helps the client to restructure the stories and to seek new possibilities. The therapist does not behave like an expert on issues, rather acts as a skillful facilitator who seeks to help the client enhance and explore understanding and potential. Together, the client and the therapist co-write the new chapter for the client's story. According to Franklin and Jordan (1999), as one of the postmodern approaches to therapy, narrative therapy incorporates stances such as collaborating, not knowing, curiosity, and reflecting. The therapist attempts to have managed but non-constricting conversations that allow opening space for change, use tentativeness to invite new thoughts, and employ the both/and stance instead of the either/or stance to value diversity and co-existing ideas. The therapists use stories and narratives to assist the client to expand meanings and understanding.

Psychoeducational Family Practice. Psychoeducational Family Practice uses didactic presentations along with other techniques, such as cognitive-behavioral techniques and social skills training to work with families particularly on mental health, health, and substance abuse related concerns. Its purpose is to furnish relevant information, provide emotional support, and develop new skills for the target families. Psychoeducational activities are often delivered in a group setting with more than one family. Educational activities are augmented with appropriate family therapy to address individual family concerns. Psycoeducational family practice employs the strength perspective and aims to empower families to adequately handle their situations.

Family Preservation Practice. Family Preservation is an intensive practice model that focuses on strengthening the family and preventing placement of children. The model is home-based and family-centered, requiring the social worker to work effectively within the family ecological system. Life skills development in a supportive environment is vital to the success of the families that have experienced abuse or neglect. The therapist is the family's case manager and teacher who uses available resources and support to ensure the safety of the children, to prevent unnecessary placement, and to improve family functioning. Reasonable efforts are exercised to keep the family together.

Working with Groups

Groups can be viewed as multiperson systems that encompass the interaction between two or more people (Zastrow, 2001). Examples of multiperson group systems include recreational, educational, therapeutic, and personal growth groups. The family is a special case of the multiperson system because it includes primary group relationships that are often long term. These attributes are not found in other small group systems.

Johnson (1994) defines the group as a social system that is "comprised of two or more persons who have something in common and who use face-to-face interaction to share commonalty and work to fulfill common needs and solve common problems, their own and others" (p. 193).

Groups have boundaries that separate them from other systems. Groups include relationships and encompass roles that fulfill needs of group members. Groups include bonds that hold individuals together. Finally, group functioning is a complex process influenced by the actions of group members. Social workers have been using groups as a mean of intervention to meet clients' various needs. Rivas and Toseland (2001) define group work as "Goal-directed activity with small treatment and task groups aimed at meeting socioemotional needs and accomplishing tasks. This activity is directed to individual members of a group and to the group as a whole within a system of service delivery" (p. 12).

Different social group work authors classify groups into different categories. Zastrow (2001) categorizes groups into "social conversation, recreation/skill building, education, task, problem solving and decision making, focus, self-help, socialization, therapeutic, and sensitivity and encounter" (p. 6). Rivas and Toseland (2001) classify two major types of groups: treatment and task. Treatment groups include support group, educational group, growth group, therapy group, and socialization group. Task groups may range from team, committee, social action group, to coalition and council. In this chapter, groups are organized broadly into recreational, educational, therapeutic, and personal growth groups.

Recreational Groups

The goal of this group is for group members to have pure enjoyment. They do not have leaders and activities are typically spontaneous. Examples of this kind of group include playground activities, recreation center activities, and ballgames. The recreational group is viewed as a system that prevents juvenile delinquency and builds character. The popular "Midnight Basketball" activity is designed to take youngsters off the street at nighttime, bring them into organized sports, and help them stay out of trouble with the laws and the criminal elements. Team sports and other organized activities in service centers such as youth centers aim to help participants develop social skills, pursue positive leisure activities, and promote other social and personal development.

Educational Groups

The goal of this small group system is to help participants acquire knowledge and learn new skills. Leaders of this form of group are usually well-trained professionals. Educational groups focus on a variety of topics including training foster parents, teaching parenting techniques, and training volunteers for specialized functions within human service systems.

Therapeutic Groups

Group therapy is an advanced form of group work that attempts to deal with unconscious motivation and personality change of group members. Group therapy is often of long-term duration and includes clients with emotional difficulties. Group therapy is conducted by social workers in schools, institutions, or mental health centers. Social work practitioners leading group therapy are expected to have advanced knowledge and skills in small group intervention.

Personal Growth Groups

This form of group is often composed of people who wish to improve their lives through personal development. They seek to improve communication skills, develop leadership skills, improve relationship skills, and develop personal attributes. They encourage growth by helping group members to reassess their potential and to act positively on this reassessment. Examples of personal growth groups include the encounter groups

(Lieberman, Yalom, and Miles, 1973; Rogers, 1970) and integrity groups (Mowrer, 1973).

Group dynamics are critical to the positive functioning of groups. Back in 1952, Cartwright (p. 392) identified eight principles onto group dynamics that are still valid for today's practice in facilitating group functioning.

1. Groups will only be successful as a medium of change, if individuals who are to change can exert influence for change and have a feeling of belonging.
2. The greater the attractiveness of the group to the individual, the greater the influence of the group on members.
3. When attempting to change attitudes, values, or behaviors of group members, the more relevant they are to the group members, the greater the influence they can have on the members.
4. The greater the prestige of a group member in the eyes of other members, the more influence he or she will have on the group.
5. Efforts aimed at changing group members are successful when the person is pressurized to conform to group norms and standards. The deviant group member must realize deviation will result in rejection or expulsion from the group.
6. Strong pressures aimed at change can be established by creating a shared perception of group members for the need for change; the pressure for change comes from within the group.
7. Information that focuses on the need for change must be shared, and must be shared by all group members.
8. Change in one part of the group can produce stress in other parts of the group; this process can only be eliminated by reducing change efforts or by bringing about readjustments within the group.

Rivas and Toseland (2001) distinguish between treatment groups and task groups. The treatment group's "major purpose is to meet members' socioemotional needs" (p. 15). On the other hand, the task group is "to accomplish a goal that will affect a broader constituency, not just the members of the group" (p. 5).

Both types of groups are also different in their various characteristics. Common needs and situations bond members of a treatment group together, while assignments and goal attainment bond task group members together. In a treatment group, the members' roles tend to evolve out of the flexible group process and through their communications to each other. However, roles in a task group are often pre-assigned and communications are often toward the group leader in a more formalized procedure. Understandably, there are more self-disclosures and a higher demand for maintaining confidentiality within a treatment group. Task group demands much less self-disclosures and often group proceeding is not confidential.

Rivas and Toseland (2001) further list the various types of treatment and task groups. There are many categories of treatment groups: support group, education group, growth group, therapy group, and socialization group. Similarly, there are many types of task groups: teams, treatment conference, staff development, committees, cabinets, board of directors, social action groups, coalitions, and delegate councils.

Working with Communities

A systems approach to social work practice views the community as a client system that must be considered critical to social intervention regardless of the level of intervention. That is, for example, family treatment cannot be effective unless the practitioner includes the community and its various subsystems in the total treatment process of the family.

Brueggemann (1996) defines communities as "human associations based on ties of kinship, relationship, and/or shared experiences in which individuals voluntarily attempt to provide meaning in their lives, meet needs, and accomplish personal goals" (p. 110). People who are part of a community must have their basic needs and expectations met if communities are to flourish. An ecological perspective suggests that patterns and forms of groups including the family, organization, and communities contribute to individual behavior. However, individuals are not passive recipients of this input from the larger social ecology; through transaction, individuals are shaped by their environments and they in turn affect their environments. Therefore, individual social functioning can never be fully understood unless the practitioner includes the impact of the environment on the person. Furthermore, the environment must always be viewed as a series of sub systems that are made up of individuals interacting with each other. What this means is there is mutuality between individuals and ultimately between the systems that make up the larger community (Blocher and Briggs, 1983).

Blocher and Briggs (1983) believe that even though communities are conservative social systems that have a tendency to direct most activities at maintenance of the status quo, social workers use a number of change strategies in community settings including democratic participation, collaborative activities, and task-oriented social change.

Democratic Participation

The goal of practice at the community level should be to create the "competent community" (Isoce, 1974). One of the most effective ways to provide people with a feeling of ownership in change activities is through democratic participation. By incorporating community members' input through the democratic process, change is more likely to occur. Involvement in community planning activities enriches community members and better prepares them for meeting future community needs. Social workers must realize that efforts to change communities will only be successful if they are grounded in democratic values.

Successful community planning and organizing processes involve existing community leaders and trigger the development of new community leadership. People are mobilized to take responsibility for themselves and, in general, make greater contributions to the larger community.

Collaborative Activities

Collaborative activities are based on discussion and interaction among those who will be affected by social change. Collaborative activities make the democratic process work. A goal of the social worker involved in community change efforts should be to involve individuals and groups with similar interest in the collaborative process. The agreements that emerge from this kind of collaboration become the guiding principle for shaping community change efforts. Change efforts are seldom successful if imposed from above, or through "top down" efforts. This kind of process often does not take into account the needs and interest of community members most affected by the change.

Social workers have the skills, knowledge, and expertise to facilitate collaboration among those who wish to bring about change. Their knowledge of human behavior and social environment as well as social policy prepares them well for working effectively with individuals and organizations involved in collaborative efforts. Social workers also understand the importance of communicating genuine respect to community members, and that humility is important to successful community change efforts.

Task-Oriented Social Change

Another basic principle of the democratic approach to social change is the task-oriented activities. This process of planned social change at the community level is focused on the nature of the problem to be resolved and the human needs to be met. Social changes are to be evolved through engagement in agreed upon goal-oriented activities and the attainment of a sense of accomplishment through participation in successful and unsuccessful attempts. Given the fact that vested interest groups often wish to maintain the status quo within the community, a task-oriented social change effort may be perceived as threatening. Practitioners must be prepared to engage differentially and skillfully with these powerful vested interest groups. Task oriented approach in community intervention could start with identifying problems as perceived by the community members, seeking additional inputs and involvement from community members, narrowing down specific problems, identifying and prioritizing achievable problem-solving objectives, anticipating barriers and preparing responses, implementing interventions, and evaluating results.

It is a democratic process that is grounded on the position that social planning is better developed with a "bottom up" approach. Community members who become involved in task-oriented social change efforts will probably develop strong emotional identification with the change process. This identification can be a very powerful tool for the subsequent change actions.

Resistance to Social Change

Planning for social change at the macro level is similar to promoting change at the micro level. Intervention at both levels should involve democratic principles such as participation and self-determination. Just as the individual in counseling, the community as a client system may not be receptive to change. The practitioner grounded in the ecological perspective realizes these kinds of phenomena are typical of systems in general, including individual clients (Blocher and Briggs, 1983).

Interventions in the community create disequilibrium and its associated stress within the community. The community must adjust to this tension and certain members may feel uncomfortable or resist the change. Blocher and Briggs (1983) contend even self-renewal at the macro level is often resisted because the community aims most of its energy at maintenance rather than change.

One of the challenges for social workers in community practice is to insulate themselves from being discouraged. The planned rational change that the practitioner is advocating for in the community may not be viewed as feasible or is often resisted. In addition to being patient and committed to the democratic process, practitioners must also become skillful in working with resistant client systems and not be deterred by the intensity of the resistance.

As Watson (1967) points out, human behavior is naturally resistant to change. Individuals are the building blocks of the community. Individuals seek stability; communities seek stability. Stability is built on habit and continuity in one's everyday life. Community social change efforts challenge the status quo, resistance to change efforts is consequently inevitable.

The Responsive Community

Responsive communities have unique characteristics that produce ecosystems that nurture individual self-actualization. The following conditions that create the responsive community are adapted from the work of Blocher and Briggs (1983).

Vision. The responsive community provides opportunities for community members to create new visions for overcoming obstacles that have stifled development in the past. For this to occur, the environment must offer novelty, complexity, ambiguity, and emotional intensity that stimulate persons to action. When high levels of stimulation from the environment occur, some individuals will withdraw, but others will respond in a positive fashion. Static communities do not offer the environmental stimulation to change; thus the role of the social worker is to create visions of change in community members that move people to action. Extremely restrictive subsystems in the community, for example, static school systems, do not offer the stimulation for change. The practitioner must work with subsystems such as schools because they are key change agents for developing responsive communities. Special programs for children such as Head Start have been an effective change agent. The critical strategy for the practitioner is to help create visions of change in critical subsystems that will eventually impact the entire community.

Participation. Meaningful participation by community members in change efforts is critical to the growth and development of the community and its members. Participation in community change means taking responsibility for their own lives. There are many prejudgments about the oppressed communities, particularly the poor and the minorities. It is critical for the practitioner to mobilize oppressed people in community change efforts through meaningful participation.

Resources. Community practice social workers are skillful brokers who could identify and link the needed resources to meet the changing demands of the community and its members. Resources of support are not only material, but also psychological, such as providing empathy, care, and other similar kinds of support. Providing these kinds of support to community members involved in change efforts can lead to individual growth and development, and ultimately to the responsive community.

Strategy. Strategies based on clear, consistent, and rational expectations guide the process aimed at changing communities. This kind of information provides community members involved in change efforts with a point of reference, and helps to insure that they will act in a coordinated fashion.

Evaluation. Another aspect of the process aimed at developing the responsive community is to evaluate the change effort. Evaluation not only provides information for the results of the intervention but also indicators for developing future efforts in developing the responsive community.

EMPIRICAL-BASED INTERVENTIONS

There are many empirical-based interventions. Among them are the behavioral and cognitive therapeutic intervention approaches. Both interventions compliment the ecosystem-oriented assessment-intervention approach (Pardeck, 1996), a model that will be discussed shortly as one of the alternative approaches for social work practice.

Behavioral Intervention

There are many theorists who are associated with behaviorism which was introduced by John B. Watson. Ivan Pavlov conducted the famous conditioned-reflex experiment helped explain how people learn. B. F. Skinner (1953) believed that most emotions are conditioned by habit and that they could be learned and unlearned through a systematic approach of behavioral modification. Skinner did not develop new principles of behaviorism, instead he translated the theories and ideas of other behaviorists into an applied and useful therapeutic technology.

From a behavioral perspective, individuals are viewed as biological entities that respond to the events that happen to them. In essence, people are largely products of their environment. They are responders to their environments; these environments shape both functional and dysfunctional behaviors.

From an intervention point of view, social workers who use a behavioral approach adopt a stimulus response paradigm. Clients are seen as entities that respond in a predictable fashion to any given stimulus according to what they have learned through past experience.

Skinner views people as catalogued with a repertoire of responses that are repeated over and over. Specifically, people learn specific responses that satisfy environmental conditions. Individual behavior is predictable and environmental conditions play a central role in determining behavior. Given this principle, the role of the social worker is one of helping clients to unlearn and to replace dysfunctional behaviors and to promote change in the environment. Behavioral intervention is a re-education or re-learning process in which positive behaviors are reinforced and unhelpful behaviors extinguished. Through reinforcement principles, the client learns functional behaviors, and unlearns dysfunctional behaviors.

Social workers who do client assessment through a behavioral approach follow the basic steps of: identifying the presenting problem, determining the cause of the problem, and selecting a solution. The solution or intervention will involve positive reinforcement of functional behaviors and the elimination of undesired behaviors. Some behavioral problems are typically viewed as rooted in antecedents and consequences; these processes thus become the focus of intervention.

There are a number of techniques in applying behavioral intervention. These include contingency contracting, self-management, shaping, biofeedback, and modeling. One of the goals of intervention for the service provider is to help the client learn strategies for coping. From a philosophical viewpoint all behavior can be changed, the task is finding the appropriate positive or negative stimuli to accomplish this goal. Numerous techniques are available to reduce or eliminate anxiety, obsessive behaviors, phobias, depression, and other problematic behaviors. Another goal of behavioral intervention is to teach clients self-management skills that they can apply to other life situations. Through this approach clients learn to become their own behavioral modification experts.

Krumboltz and Hosford (1967) and Krumboltz (1966) have identified four main categories for organizing goals of behavioral intervention: 1. alerting maladaptive behavior; 2. teaching the decision-making process; 3. preventing problems; and 4. teaching new behaviors and skills.

Behaviorists are sensitive to what is referred to as the intra-self; however, since this intra-self cannot be seen directly, they prefer to work with observable results of these internal psychological processes. The guiding principle behind this position is that if the symptoms can be changed (overt behavior), the internal psychological causes are of secondary importance. In other words, what is critical to the behaviorist is changing those activities that contribute to problems, and not necessarily their cause.

The nature and structure of behavioral approaches allow them to be more adapted to empirical studies. Behaviorist theorists were the first to mount a significant challenge to psychodynamic models that were widely used prior to the development of behavioral approaches. Social workers who use a behavioral approach would likely find themselves more ready and able to document and assess their practice effectiveness.

Cognitive Therapeutic Intervention

The focus of cognitive therapy is on psychological disturbances caused by aberrations in thinking. The role of the therapist is to help clients develop psychological skills to correct this condition. Therapeutic skills include labeling and interpreting negative psychological disturbances and ultimately correcting these conditions through therapy. There are a number of therapists who represent the cognitive therapeutic approach including Aaron Beck (1976), William Glasser (1969), and Albert Ellis (1975).

Cognitive therapy expects clients to have the capacity for introspection and reflection on their thoughts and feelings. Therapeutic activities are aimed at increasing client self-awareness. The goal of this process is for clients to substitute accurate judgments for inaccurate judgments. However, not all clients have the cognitive or intellectual capacity to engage in this form of therapy (Ellis, 1975).

Ellis views human beings as largely irrational beings that need to be taught rational approaches for dealing with problems. Humans think crookedly about their desires and preferences and this results in anger, anxiety, depression, and self-pity. Unfortunately, irrational thinking leads to self-hate, which may lead to self-destructive behavior and eventually to hatred of others. Ellis (1975) believes some irrational thoughts are biological in origin but most result from the socialization process.

The goal of Ellis' rational-emotive therapy is to teach people to think and behave in a more functional fashion. Furthermore, people must take responsibility for the self, including their own logical thinking and the behaviors that result from their thinking.

Evidence-Based Practice

During the past decade, evidence-based practice has attracted much attention from medical and human service professionals. There has been a noticeable increase in literature on the topic among professionals such as medicine, nursing, social work, and psychology (Gibbs, 2003).

Evidence-based practice was originated by the medical group at McMaster University in Canada (Evidence-based Medicine Working Group, 1992). Gibbs (2003) describes evidence-based practice as "a process, not a collection of truths. This process involves posing specific questions of practical value to clients, searching electronically for the current best evidence, and taking action guided by that evidence" (p. 19). It is an integration of values, experience, common sense, and evidence.

Operationally, Gibbs incorporates the steps suggested by the McMaster University group and proposes seven major steps for engaging in evidence-based practices (pp. 8–9):

1. Becoming motivated to apply evidence-based practice.
2. Converting information needs into a well-formulated answerable question.
3. Tracking down with maximum efficiency the best evidence with which to answer the question.
4. Critically appraising the evidence for its validity and usefulness.
5. Applying the results of this evidence appraisal to policy practice.
6. Evaluating performance.
7. Teaching others to do the same.

Corcoran (2003) believes that evidence-based practice "involves a process of locating research findings through electronic searches in a particular problem area to decide the intervention that has the best available support" (p. 4). Corcoran further asserts that to aid the decision on whether one approach is better than another for a particular problem area, the use of scientific experimental designs to evaluate practice effectiveness is highly encouraged.

Evidence-based practice can be incorporated into existing practice models for various types of problems. Corcoran (2003) demonstrates such utilities of evidence-based practice in working with families in diverse settings and with various problems. She incorporates the evidence-based approach in family therapeutic models including psychoeducation intervention, behavioral parent training, solution-focused therapy, cognitive-behavioral intervention, structural family therapy, and multisystemic treatment in working with clients of different ages and problems.

The rise of evidence-based social work practice in recent years certainly reflects the reality of increased demand for accountability and outcomes by managed care systems and other funding sources. It also echoes the

profession's desire for developing practice models and knowledge that are rooted in scientific inquiry and guided by proven evidence.

ECOSYSTEM-ORIENTED ASSESSMENT-INTERVENTION APPROACH

This framework of the ecosystem-oriented assessment-intervention approach (Pardeck, 1996) is an example of an empirically based practice model. This model is adapted from the field of community psychology (Plas, 1981). It involves seven stages and can be used in a variety of practice settings. The model does not necessarily deviate a great deal from traditional approaches to assessment and intervention in terms of data gathering, but rather in the way that the practitioner conceptualizes and organizes the assessment and intervention process. The seven stages are as follows:

1. Entering the system
2. Mapping the ecology
3. Assessing the ecology
4. Creating the vision and the specific plan for change
5. Coordinating-communicating
6. Reassessing
7. Evaluating.

Entering the System

Once the decision is made to offer services to a client, the first step the practitioner takes is to enter the ecosystem of the client. This process involves two major steps: (1) assessment of the relationships in the client's life, and (2) identification of a point of entry into the client's world.

Assessing the relationships of the client involves focusing on the subsystems that shape the client's world; these include the family, the school, and the community. The practitioner gathers critical input from these subsystems that will guide the intervention process. The next step for the practitioner is to find a point of entry into the client's world. This can be accomplished through interviews involving the client and his or her family or immediate support systems. This might be accomplished through attending an already scheduled parent and teacher conference for the child. Through assessing the various subsystems in the client's world, the practitioner attempts to identify sources of discord in the client's ecosystem as well as strengths.

Mapping the Ecology

After the practitioner enters the client's world, the next step involves the process of mapping the ecology. Systems analysis is a critical strategy during this stage. The various subsystems of the client's world are explored by the practitioner so as to identify the people and events that are pertinent to the presenting problem(s) of the client.

Important subsystems related to the client can be classified under two broad categories of people and events. Events of importance include those considered to be typical occasions within the client's world that support either positive or negative behaviors and feelings. For example, during an interview, the husband of the client may make the following comments: "Whenever she is around her mother, she acts as if I don't exist ... When we are away from her mother, our relationship seems to be fuller."

Identification of people and events can be accomplished through a number of approaches, including structured interviews with the client and significant persons in the client's life. A fine number of empirically based assessment instruments have been created by social workers and other human service professionals. Examples of these instruments are listed at the end of this chapter. Hudson (1992), in particular, has created a number of scales that can be used to assess relationships in family systems. These instruments are the *Index of Family Relations*, *Child's Attitude Toward Mother*, *Child's Attitude Toward Father*, and *Parental Attitude Scale*. Besides, there are many interactive and practical approaches such as Genogram, Ecomap, and family sculpturing, which are useful for mapping out client's situation and major concerns.

Assessing the Ecology

Once the ecology has been mapped, the data gathered must be interpreted. At this point, the practitioner is searching for the primary problems and the major areas of strength in the client's ecosystem. An important component of this stage is to describe relationships and recurring themes in the client's ecosystem. Relationships between influential events and influential persons present at those events need to be explored and recurring themes need to be recorded. For example, is the same person, or group of persons, always present at those events, which are deemed critical? Which events are viewed as influential by the significant persons in the client's ecosystem? Then the practitioner would prioritize or weigh these relationships according to their importance in maintaining the ecosystem of the client as well as in the possibilities for changing it.

The process is designed to elicit data concerning those people and situations that support useful behaviors and those that support negative actions and feelings. Once the strengths, weaknesses, and critical relationships have been identified, the practitioner can present this information to the client and significant persons in the client's ecosystem.

Creating the Vision and Specific Plan for Change

At this point in the process, the benefits of assessing and mapping the ecology begin to be realized. This phase of the intervention process should try to include the significant individuals in the client's ecosystem who can influence change. With meaningful involvement from the clients and their significant individuals, areas that need to be changed and strategies to achieve these changes are identified and prioritized.

When focusing on the changes needed, it is important that the practitioner considers the total ecosystem of the client and builds on the strengths present in this ecology. The practitioner should be sensitive to all possibilities of change. When clear objectives and strategies for change are identified, then the key activities are to implement and monitor the intervention process.

Coordinating–Communicating

An important activity of the practitioner during the intervention process is to coordinate and communicate with those in the client's ecosystem. For the most part, much of the change efforts rely on the client and those significant persons in the client's ecosystem. The practitioner has the coordinating and communicating functions of offering support and facilitates the continuing change efforts. They are done through therapeutic counseling and case managing functions such as home visits, monitoring and brokering for service, and other supportive efforts. Given that the client's ecosystem is dynamic, the practitioner must be prepared to modify and change the intervention efforts as needed.

Re-assessing

Based on the changes agreed upon by the client and the significant persons in the client's ecosystem, the practitioner may also consider the need to re-map the client's ecosystem and work out the various stages of the intervention process. Reassessing is to study the attainment of the intervention objectives and modify them to meet the changing dynamics of the clients' environment. If the intervention efforts are assessed to be successful, the practitioner can move toward the termination process with the client and other significant persons in the client's ecosystem.

Evaluation

While the re-assessment phase is concerned with outcomes, this final stage of intervention is concerned with the evaluation of the entire intervention process. The practitioner can gather information through informal meetings with the client and others relevant to the treatment process. This evaluation can also be done through a structured questionnaire and other research technologies.

A Case Example. Gary, a two-year-old boy, was underdeveloped both physically and intellectually. The child's vocabulary consisted of approximately three words and he was not able to walk more than two steps without assistance. The child was diagnosed as having fetal alcohol syndrome. The symptoms included syndactyly (fusion of the fingers) of the middle and ring fingers bilaterally, and other evidences of fetal alcohol syndrome. Gary's parents were both alcoholics and unemployed when Gary was placed in foster care. The family was not receiving any kind of public assistance.

The worker assigned to Gary's case had his first opportunity to enter the ecosystem of Gary during a two-hour home visit with his parents, while a number of relatives were also present. The worker observed the interaction patterns between Gary and the family. During the home visit, the worker began the stage of mapping the ecology of Gary's family system. The worker concluded that Gary's parents did not interact with him in a typical fashion. The mother in particular held the child for no more than two minutes during the home visit, the father did not interact with the child at all. When the child was not playing on the floor, he was passed from one relative to the next. The mother commented several times during the home visit about how curious Gary had always been about "things" in his environment and how active the child was.

One week after the visit, the worker did an extensive interview with each of the parents and one of the relatives present at the home visit a week earlier, gathering information that helped to assess the ecological system of the child and the interventions needed to help Gary return to his biological family. Through the interview, the worker learned that both parents continued to abuse alcohol; this was confirmed by Gary's parents and the relative interviewed. It was also learned that Gary's father was working part-time and had not reported his income to the Welfare

Department. The worker viewed the fact that Gary's father was working as a strength even though the income earned was not reported.

The next step, creating the vision of change, involved a number of services and persons in Gary's ecosystem. The worker had to coordinate each of these services to insure that the change effort was being followed through. It was decided that Gary should continue in an agreed upon foster care for two more months before his case would be reviewed. Plans for change were developed for Gary and his parents. During this time, Gary would go into a special treatment program that would be aimed at increasing Gary's motor and intellectual development. As the child was underweight and in the lower fifth percentile in height, regular visits to a medical doctor were suggested. The worker also advised the foster parents to provide a stimulating environment for the child as much as possible.

Gary's parents agreed to enroll in a treatment program for their alcohol problem and participate in parenting classes. They were linked with other social services in the community to better meet their other service needs. The worker closely monitored the parent's activities to ensure that they followed through on the intervention plan. An effort was made to help Gary's father find a full-time job. The coordinating communicating stage was accomplished through telephone calls, in person contacts, and home visits. The parents also agreed that when Gary visited each week for two hours they would not have relatives present. This strategy will allow the worker to better assess how the parents alone interacted with Gary.

After two months the re-assessment stage began. Gary's motor and intellectual development had shown improvement through the efforts of the specialized treatment program and of the foster parents. Gary was now able to walk alone and had a significant increase in his vocabulary as reflected by the worker's observation and the foster parents' report. Through self-report and service record reviews, it was concluded that Gary's mother had followed through on her counseling for alcoholism; however, his father had missed a number of sessions. Gary's parents had also attended parenting classes on a regular basis. Gary's father found full-time employment. As the income earned by Gary's father was extremely low, the family was eligible for a number of supplemental services including low rent housing. During Gary's weekly two-hour home visits, only Gary's parents were present, and the worker observed much improvement in their interaction. Subsequently, adequate housing was obtained by the family, and the family continued to receive an array of support. It was the opinion of the alcohol counselor that Gary's mother was making great progress, however, she was not deemed ready for Gary to return home. There was also some concern about Gary's father not attending counseling on a regular basis. The professionals working with Gary, including the medical doctor, felt that Gary should continue to receive specialized treatment to improve his physical and emotional development. Thus it was decided that Gary should continue in foster care for two additional months. Gary's parents agreed to the revised plan that they would continue counseling, home visits would occur on a weekly basis for two hours, and Gary would continue receiving the necessary treatment. The final evaluation step was not implemented because intervention efforts were still in process. However, ongoing evaluation and monitoring had been in place since the first meeting with the clients.

ASSESSMENT INSTRUMENTS FOR SOCIAL WORK PRACTICE

Accurate assessment is important for effective social work practice (Wodarski, 1981). Accurate assessment is also critical to the successful use of the ecosystem-oriented assessment-intervention approach in social work practice. A number of assessment instruments are currently available that involve little time, energy, or cost to administer. These instruments are designed to measure various factors critical to conducting an analysis of a client's presenting condition. They are designed to conduct assessment at the individual, family, and environmental levels. Many of these tools are also available in computer format, which increases their ease of use for practice. The following reviews a variety of assessment instruments currently available that will help facilitate assessment and treatment. Social workers may wish to consider the application of some of the appropriate instruments under suitable service contexts and clinical considerations.

The instruments presented include behavior rating scales, self-report inventories, structured interviews, and observational coding systems. Behavior rating scales are completed by an informed source in reference to behavioral characteristics of a client system including a family system, whereas self-report inventories are completed by the client system. Behavior rating scales and self-report inventories are easier to administer than the structured interview or direct observation. Behavior rating scales and self-report inventories provide empirical information about the success of an intervention.

Standardized questions and responses are a part of the structured interview that provides extensive information on a client's social functioning. Observational coding systems involve observing and recording of certain behaviors and events in a naturalistic or structured situation. This approach involves a great deal of time and effort on the part of the practitioner.

Using and Selecting Instruments

For an instrument to effectively assess a presenting problem of a client, the instrument must have acceptable levels of reliability and validity. This means it consistently measures what it claims to measure and that it does so with a great degree of accuracy.

The practitioner should become familiar with any assessment instrument prior to its use. Basic information on each instrument listed in this chapter is offered, including what the instrument measures and the kind of client population the instrument is used to make assessments about.

When the practitioner uses assessment instruments, the client must give his or her informed consent. The client should be told what the instrument assesses and who will see the information generated from the assessment. If the practitioner keeps these important points in mind, the instruments should increase practice effectiveness.

Adolescent Alcohol Involvement Scale (Mayer and Filstead, 1979). This 14-item self-report inventory categorizes adolescent alcohol use/abuse along a continuum from abstinence to misuse. It has demonstrated high test–retest reliability in screening adolescent populations for alcohol misuse.

Adult–Adolescent Parenting Inventory (Bavolek, 1984). This is a 32-item self-report inventory aimed at measuring parenting strengths and weaknesses in four areas: inappropriate developmental expectations, lack of empathy toward children's needs, belief in use of corporal punishment, and reversal of parent–child roles. The client responds to each item on a five-point scale (from "strongly agree" to "strongly disagree").

Attitude Toward the Provision of Long-Term Care (Klein, 1992). This 26-item self-report inventory, rated on a one-to-five continuum, assesses attitudes toward the provision of informal long-term care for family members.

Beck Depression Inventory (Beck, 1967). This consists of a 21-item self-report inventory widely used in clinical practice for measuring depression. Clients indicate on a scale from zero to three the severity of their current symptoms.

Behavior Problem Checklist (Quay, 1977). This 55-item behavior-rating scale assesses the types and degree of behavioral problems in children and adolescents. The practitioner completes the three-point scale. The scale consists of four subscales including identifying conduct problems, personality problems, inadequacy-immaturity, and socialized delinquency.

Child Abuse Potential Survey (Milner, Gold, Ayoub, and Jacewitz, 1984). This 160-item self-report inventory, completed by a parent, is designed to be used as a screening device to differentiate physical abusers from non-abusers. Factors assessed include distress, rigidity, child with problems, problems from family and others, unhappiness, loneliness, and negative concepts of child and self. Respondents are asked either to agree or disagree with each item.

Child Behavior Checklist (Achenbach and Edelbrock, 1979). This is a 118-item behavioral-rating scale widely used to measure problem behaviors of children. The practitioner rates a variety of behaviors on a three-point scale. These include the checklist measures for internalizing syndromes (i.e., depression, immaturity) and externalizing syndromes (i.e., aggression, hyperactivity).

Child Well-Being Scales (Magura and Moses, 1986). These 43-item behavior-rating scales are a multidimensional measure of child maltreatment situations specifically designed for use as an outcome measure in child protective services programs rather than for individual cases. The scales focus on actual or potential unmet needs of children. Current testing of the subscales indicates that three factors (household adequacy, 10 scales; parental disposition, 14 scales; and child performance, 4 scales) accounted for 43 percent variance and that the Child Well-Being Scale can discriminate between neglectful and non-neglectful families. It requires approximately 25 minutes for the practitioner to complete and is based on direct contact with the family, including in-home visits. Each dimension is rated on a three- or six-point continuum of adequacy/inadequacy.

Child's Attitudes Toward Father (CAF) (Hudson, 1992). This 25-item self-report inventory, rated on a one-to-seven continuum, measures the degree, severity, and magnitude of problems a child has with his or her father.

Child's Attitudes Toward Mother (CAM) (Hudson, 1992). This 25-item self-report inventory, rated on a one-to-seven continuum, measures the degree, severity, and magnitude of problems a child has with his or her mother.

Childhood Level of Living Scale (Polansky, Chalmers, Buttenwieser, and Williams, 1981). This 99-item behavior-rating scale assesses neglect of children up to 7 years of age. The nine subscales include: general positive child care, state of repair of home, negligence, quality of household maintenance, quality of health care and grooming, encouragement of competence, inconsistency of discipline and coldness, encouragement of superego development, and material giving. It requires approximately 15 minutes for the practitioner who knows the family well to answer all items "yes" or "no."

Children's Beliefs About Parental Divorce Scale (CBAPDS) (Kurdek and Berg, 1987). This 36-item assessment scale is designed to measure children's beliefs about their parents' divorce. The instrument uses a yes/no response format. It is designed for children aged 8 to 14.

Children's Cognitive Assessment Questionnaire (CCAQ) (Zatz and Chassing, 1983). This 40-item assessment instrument measures self-defeating and self-enhancing cognition associated with test anxiety and is useful for practitioners working in school or residential settings. It consists of a true/false format for each item and is designed for children aged 9 to 12.

Children's Depression Inventory (Kovacs, 1981). This 27-item self-report inventory is a modified version of the *Beck Depression Inventory*. It measures overt symptoms of childhood depression including sadness, suicidal ideation, and sleep and appetite disturbances. The inventory is designed for children aged 8 to 14. The child responds to a three-point scale for each item.

Children's Perceived Self-Control (CPSC) Scale (Humphrey, 1982). This 11-item scale measures self-control from a cognitive-behavioral perspective. It is designed for children 8 to 12 years of age. The scale addresses interpersonal self-control, personal self-control, and self-evaluation and uses a "usually yes" or "usually no" format for each item.

Co-Dependency Inventory (CODI) (Stonebrink, 1988). This 29-item instrument is designed to assess codependency in family and friends of substance abusers. Codependency is defined as enabling the abuser to continue to use chemicals and/or trying to control the abuser's use of alcohol and/or drugs. The client responds to items on a four-point continuum.

Conflict Tactics Scale (Straus, 1979). This 19-item self-report inventory is used to assess conflict among family members. A parent or child responds to a six-point scale (from "never" to "more than 20 times") to indicate the number of times in the past year that specific techniques were used during family conflict.

Dyadic Adjustment Scale (Spanier and Filsinger, 1983). This 32-item self-report inventory consists of three different types of rating responses measuring satisfaction in intimate relationships.

Depression Self-Rating Scale (DSRS) (Birleson, 1981). This scale assesses the extent and severity of depression in children. The instrument consists of 18 items and assesses depression in children between the ages of 7 and 13. The instrument includes items on a three-point scale that assesses mood, physiological and somatic complaints, and cognitive aspects of depression.

Developmental Profile II (Alpern, Boll, and Shearer, 1980). This 186-item behavioral-rating scale assesses the functioning of children from birth to age 9 in five areas including physical, self-help, social, academic, and communication. The items are rated either "pass" or "fail." The scale can be completed in 20 to 40 minutes by a practitioner employing knowledge of the child's skills, observations, and/or parent interviews.

Generalized Contentment Scale (Hudson, 1992). This 25-item self-report inventory, rated in a one-to-seven continuum, measures the degree, severity, and magnitude of nonpsychotic depression and focuses largely on affective aspects of depression.

Dyadic Parent–Child Interaction Coding System (Robinson and Eyberg, 1981). This observational assessment tool assesses the interaction of parents and young conduct-problem children. Parent and child are observed during 15-minute segments as they interact in three structured clinical situations.

Environmental Assessment Index (EAI) (Poresky, 1987). This 44-item index (or 22-item short form) is designed to assess the educational/developmental quality of children's home environments. A practitioner scores each 'yes' or 'no' item based on either direct observation or information from the child's parent.

Family Adaptability and Cohesion Evaluation Scales (FACES III) (Olson, 1986). FACES III is a 40-item self-report assessing the cohesion and adaptability of family functioning. Cohesion is defined as the degree of emotional bonding between family members; adaptability is defined as the ability of the family system to change its power structure, roles, and rules in response to environmental stress.

Family Assessment Device (FAD) (Hendershot and LeClere, 1993). FAD assesses family dynamics, which include affective involvement, behavioral control, roles, problem solving, communication, and affective responsiveness.

Family Assessment Form (McCroskey, Nishimoto, and Subramanian, 1991). This observational assessment tool includes five subscales with 102 items. It assesses the family's physical, social, and economic environment; psychosocial history of caregivers; personal characteristics of caregivers; child-rearing skills; caregiver-to-child interactions; developmental status of children; and overall psychosocial functioning of the family. Family functioning is rated on a five-point scale linked to child maltreatment.

Family Assessment Measure (FAM III) (Hendershot and LeClere, 1993). FAM III assesses the following family dynamics: affective involvement, control, role performance, task accomplishment, communication, affective expression, and values and norms.

Family Environment Scale (FES) (Hendershot and LeClere, 1993). The FES assesses three dimensions of family functioning: relationships, personal growth, and systems maintenance. The relationship dimension assesses family cohesion, expression, and conflict. The personal growth dimension assesses family independence, moral-religious emphasis, and a family's achievement, intellectual-cultural, and active-recreational orientation. The systems maintenance dimension assesses the organization and control found within a family system.

Family Functioning Scale (FFS) (Hendershot and LeClere, 1993). The FFS assesses the overall functioning of a family. Five dimensions are assessed; these include: affect, family communication, family conflict, family worries, and family rituals/supports.

Family Inventory of Life Events and Changes (McCubbin and Patterson, 1983). This 71-item self-report inventory records normative and non-normative stressors a family unit may experience within a year. Family members (together or separately) respond "yes" or "no" to each item. Norms are provided for families at various stages of the family life cycle.

Family Risk Scales (Magura, Moses, and Jones, 1987). This scale consists of 26 behavioral-rating items designed to identify a full range of situations predictive of near-term child placement so that preventive services can be offered and change monitored. The scales are similar to the *Child Well-Being Scales*. Dimensions are focused on the areas that are potentially malleable.

Home Observation for Measurement of the Environment Inventory (Caldwell and Bradley, 1978). This 100-item observation/interview procedure inventory assesses the quality of stimulation of a child's early environment. There are two versions of the inventory for children aged birth to 3 and one for 3 to 6-year-olds. Approximately one third of the items are answered through a parent interview; the practitioner of the child and the primary caretaker in the home answer the remaining items on observations. It requires approximately 1 hour to answer all of the items with a "yes" or "no" response.

Implicit Parental Learning Theory Interview (Honig, Caldwell, and Tannenbaum, 1973). This 45-item, 45-minute structured interview is designed to inventory the techniques a parent uses to deal with developmentally appropriate behaviors of preschool children. Five forms are available for use with parents of children aged 1 to 4 and 5 to 6.

Index of Brother Relations (IBR) (Hudson, 1992). This 25-item self-report inventory, rated on a one-to-seven continuum, measures the degree, severity, and magnitude of problems a person has with his or her brother.

Index of Family Relations (Hudson, 1992). This instrument assesses the extent, severity, and magnitude of problems that family members experience in a family system. It offers a global assessment of family relations. It employs a 25-item self-report inventory rated on a one-to-seven continuum measuring the extent, severity, or magnitude of problems that family members have in their relationship with one another.

Index of Marital Satisfaction (Hudson, 1992). This 25-item self-report inventory, rated on a one-to-seven continuum, measures the degree, severity, and magnitude of problems with a spouse or partner.

Index of Parental Attitudes (Hudson, 1992). This 25-item self-report inventory, rated on a one-to-seven continuum, measures the extent, severity, and magnitude of parent–child relationship problems as perceived and reported by the parent in reference to a child.

Index of Peer Relationships (Hudson, 1992). This 25-item self-report inventory, rated on a one-to-seven continuum, measures the degree, severity, and magnitude of a client's problems in relationships with peers. It can be used as a global measure of peer relationship problems in a number of settings.

Index of Self-Esteem (Hudson, 1992). This 25-item self-report inventory, rated on a one-to-seven continuum, measures the degree, severity, and magnitude of a client's problem in the area of self-esteem.

Index of Sexual Satisfaction (Hudson, 1992). This 25-item self-report inventory, rated on a one-to-seven continuum, measures the degree, severity, and magnitude of sexual discord or dissatisfaction in a dyadic relationship.

Index of Sister Relations (ISR) (Hudson, 1992). This 25-item self-report inventory, rated on a one-to-seven continuum, measures the degree, severity, and magnitude of problems a person has with his or her sister.

Index of Spouse Abuse (Hudson and McIntosh, 1981). This 30-item self-report scale, rated on a one-to-five continuum, measures the severity and magnitude of physical or nonphysical abuse inflicted on a woman by her spouse or partner. Clinical cutting scores are recommended for both physical or nonphysical abuse subscale scores.

Inventory of Family Feelings (Lowman, 1980). This 38-item self-report inventory assesses the overall degree of attachment between family members. Family members respond to a three-point scale on each item.

Inventory of Socially Supportive Behaviors (Barrera, Sandler, and Ramsay, 1981). This 40-item self-report inventory assesses the frequency with which individuals have received aid and assistance from the people around them. Respondents answer each item through a five-point scale (from "not at all" to "every day").

Marital Satisfaction Inventory (Snyder, 1983). This 280-item self-report inventory assesses an individual's attitudes and beliefs regarding 11 specific areas of marital functioning. The inventory requires approximately 30 minutes for individual spouses to respond to "true" "false" items and includes subscales on dissatisfaction with children and conflict over child rearing.

Maternal Characteristics Scale (Polansky, Gaudin, and Kilpatrick, 1992). This 35-item observational rating scale consists of descriptive statements with which the practitioner assesses relatedness, impulse-control, confidence, and verbal accessibility. The practitioner responds to true or false (or mostly true/mostly false) items.

Michigan Screening Profile of Parenting (Paulson, Afifi, Chaleff, Thomason, and Liu, 1975). This 30-item self-report inventory assesses attitudes regarding child-rearing and parental self-awareness and self-control. Clients respond to each item on a seven-point scale ranging from "strongly agree" to "strongly disagree."

Multi-Problem Screening Inventory (MPSI) (Hudson, 1990). This is a 334-item self-report scale measuring 27 dimensions of family functioning. Subscales measure the following: depression, self-esteem, partner problems, sexual discord, child problems, mother problems, personal stress, friend problems, neighbor problems, school problems, aggression, work associates, family problems, suicide, nonphysical abuse, physical abuse, fearfulness, ideas of reference, phobias, guilt, work problems, confused thinking, disturbing thoughts, memory loss, alcohol abuse, and drug abuse. Questions are answered through a seven-point Likert scale (from "none of the time" to "all of the time"). The scale can be computer-scored.

Nowicki-Strickland Locus of Control Scale (N-SLCS) (Nowicki and Strickland, 1973). This 40-item scale is designed to assess a child's beliefs about chance or fate. Targeted for children 11 to 18 years of age, the scale features items requiring a "yes" or "no" response.

Parent Locus of Control Scale (PLOC) (Campis, Lyman, and Prentice-Dunn, 1986). This 47-item five-point scale is designed to assess parental locus of control relating to the parent's (internal) or child's (external) power in a given family situation. Items assess parental efficacy, parental responsibility, child's control of parents' life, parental belief in fate and chance, and parental control of child's behavior.

Parent–Adolescent Communications Inventory (Bienvenu, 1969). This 40-item self-report inventory assesses communication patterns and characteristics between parents and adolescents. Adolescents aged 13 to 19 years respond to each item using a three-point scale.

Parental Authority Questionnaire (PAQ) (Buri, 1991). This 30-item assessment tool includes a five-point scale designed to measure parental authority and disciplinary practice.

Parent-Child Behavioral Coding System (Forehand and McMahon, 1981). This observational tool assesses patterns of parent–child interaction. A practitioner codes parent and child behaviors in a 10-minute structured exercise in a clinic setting or in a 40-minute unstructured home visit.

Parenting Stress Index (Abidin, 1986). This 101-item self-report index assesses a mother's perception of stress associated with child and parent characteristics. An additional 19 optional items can be administered assessing stressful life events. Mothers complete the index in approximately 30 minutes.

Partner Abuse Scale: Non-physical (PASNP) (Hudson, 1992). This 25-item self-report inventory, rated on a one-to-seven continuum, measures the degree, severity, and magnitude of non-physical abuse from a spouse or partner.

Physical Abuse Partner Scale (PAPS) (Hudson, 1992). This 25-item self-report inventory, rated on a one-to-seven continuum, measures the degree, severity, and magnitude of physical abuse from a spouse or partner.

Problem-Oriented Screening Instrument for Teenagers (POSIT) (Rahdert, 1991). This 139-item self-report screening instrument assesses substance abuse problems, physical health status, mental health status, family relationships, peer relationships, educational status, vocational status, social skills, leisure and recreation, and aggressive behavior/delinquency. It is designed for children aged 13 to 19 years.

Provision of Social Relations (PRS) (Turner, Frankel, and Levin, 1983). This 15-item instrument is designed to assess components of social support. The items are responded to through a five-point continuum. Social support includes attachment, social integration, reassurance of worth, reliable alliance, and guidance.

Rosenberg Self-Esteem Scale (Rosenberg, 1979). This 10-item self-report inventory measures the self-esteem of children 13 to 18 years of age. The child rates each item on a four-point scale.

Self-Perception Profile for Children (Harter, 1982). This 28-item self-rating inventory assesses cognitive, social, and physical competence in children. The scale is designed for children in the 3rd through 9th grades. For each item, the child is asked to first identify which of two passages best describes the child, then the child rates whether the description is "sort of true" or "really true."

Self-Report Family Inventory (SFI) (Olson and Tiesel, 1993). The SFI is theoretically grounded in the Beavers Systems Model of Family Functioning (BSM). Two dimensions are measured: (1) overall competence and behavior of the family system and (2) emotional style used by the family system. The overall competence dimension includes family happiness, optimism, problem solving, and parental coalitions. The behavioral and emotional style dimension assesses family conflict, communication, cohesion, leadership, and emotional expression.

Social Support Behaviors Scale (Vaux, Riedel, and Stewart, 1987). This 45-item self-report inventory assesses five modes of support: emotional, socializing, practical assistance, financial assistance, and advice/guidance. Respondents record on a five-point scale (from "no one would do this" to "most family members/friends would certainly do this") the likelihood of family and friends helping in various ways.

Standardized Observation System 3 (Wahler, House, and Stambaugh, 1976). This observational tool assesses interactions between a child and other members of a family system. The practitioner codes the interactional sequence in a 1-hour unstructured home visit.

REFERENCES

Abidin, R. R. (1986). *Parenting stress index manual*. Charlottesville, VA: Pediatric Psychology Press.

Achenbach, T. M. & Edelbrock, C. S. (1979). The Child Behavior Profile: II. Boys aged 12–16 and girls aged 6–11 and 12–16. *Journal of Consulting and Clinical Psychology*, 47, 223–233.

Alpern, G. D., Boll, T. J., & Shearer, M. W. (1980). *The developmental profile II manual*. Aspen, CO: Psychological Development.

Bandura, A. (1977). *Social Learning Theory*. Englewood Cliffs, NJ: Prentice-Hall.

Barrera, M., Jr., Sandler, I. N., & Ramsay, T. B. (1981). Preliminary development of a scale of social support: Studies on college students. *American Journal of Community Psychology*, 9, 435–447.

Bavolek, S. (1984). *Handbook for the AAPI: Adult-Adolescent Parenting Inventory*. Park City, Utah: Family Development Resources, Inc.

Beck, A. (1967). *Depression: Clinical, experimental and theoretical aspects*. New York: Harper & Row.

Beck, A. (1976). *Cognitive therapy and emotional disorders*. New York: International Universities Press.

Beck, A. (1989). *Cognitive therapy and the emotional disorders*. Harmondsworth, England: Penguin.

Bienvenu, M. J. (1969). Measurement of parent-adolescent communication. *Family Coordinator*, 19, 117–121.

Birleson, P. (1981). The validity of depression disorders in childhood and the development of a self-rating scale: A research report. *Journal of Child Psychology and Psychiatry*, 22, 73–88.

Blocher, D. H. & Briggs, D. A. (1983). *Counseling psychology in community settings*. New York: Springer Publishing Company.

Bowen, M. (1978). *Family therapy in clinical practice*. New York: Aronson.

Brueggemann, W. (1996). *The practice of macro social work*. Chicago: Nelson Hall.

Buri, J. R. (1991). Parental Authority Questionnaire. *Journal of Personality and Social Assessment*, 57, 110–119.

Caldwell, B. M. & Bradley, R. H. (1978). *Home observation for measurement of the environment*. Little Rock: University of Arkansas.

Campis, L. K., Lyman, R. D., & Prentice-Dunn, S. (1986). The parental locus of control scale: Development and validation. *Journal of Clinical Child Psychiatry*, 15, 260–267.

Caplan, G. (1965). *Principles of preventive psychiatry*. London: Travistock.

Cartwright, D. (1951). Achieving change in people: Some complications of group dynamics theory. *Human Relations*, 4, 381–393.

Constable, R. & Lee, D. (2004). *Social work with families: Content and process*. Chicago: Lyceum.

Corcoran, J. (2003). Clinical applications of evidence-based family interventions. New York: Oxford University Press.

Ellis, A. (1962). *Reason and emotion in psychotherapy*. Secaucus, NJ: Lyle Stuart.

Ellis, A. (1975). The impossibility of achieving consistently good mental health. *American Psychologist*, 42, 364–375.

Epstein, L. (1992). *Brief treatment and a new look at task-center approach*. New York: MacMillan.

Erikson, E. (1963). *Childhood and society*. New York: Norton.

Evidence-Based Medicine Working Group. (1992). Evidence-based medicine. A new approach to teaching the practice of medicine. *Journal of the American Medical Association*, 268(17), 2420–2425.

Filsinger, E. E. (1983). *Marriage and family assessment. A sourcebook for family therapy*. Beverley Hill, CA: Sage.

Forehand, R. L. & McMahon, R. J. (1981). *Helping the noncompliant child: A clinician's guide to parent training*. New York: Guilford Press.

Franklin, C. & Jordan, C. (1999). *Family practice. Brief systems methods for social work*. Pacific Grove, CA: Brooks/Cole.

Germain, C. (1983). Technological advances. In A. Rosenblatt & D. Walldfogel (Eds.), *Handbook of clinical social work* (pp. 26–57). San Francisco: Jossey-Bass.

Gibbs, L. (2003). *Evidence-based practice for the helping professions: A practical guide with integrated multimedia*. Pacific Grove, CA: Brooks/Cole.

Glasser, W. (1969). *The identity society*. New York: Harper & Row.

Goldstein, H. (1990). The knowledge base of social work practice: Theory, wisdom, analogue or art? *Family in Society*, 72(1), 32-43.

Hamilton, G. (1950). *Theory and practice of social casework* (2nd ed.). New York: Columbia University Press.

Harter, S. (1982). The perceived competence scale for children. *Child Development*, 53, 87–97.

Hendershot, G. E. & LeClere, F. B. (Eds.) (1993). *Family health: From data to policy*. Minneapolis, MN: National Council on Family Relations.

Honig, A. S., Caldwell, B. M., & Tannenbaum, J. A. (1973). Maternal behavior in verbal report and in laboratory observation: A methodological study. *Child Psychiatry and Human Development*, 3, 216–230.

Hudson, W. W. (1990). *The multi-problem screening inventory*. Tempe, AZ: WALMYR.

Hudson, W. W. (1992). *The WALMYR assessment scales scoring manual*. Tempe, AZ: WALMYR

Hudson, W. W. & McIntosh, S. R. (1981). The assessment of spouse abuse: Two quantifiable dimensions. *Journal of Marriage and the Family*, 43, 873–888.

Humphrey, L. L. (1982). Children's and teachers' perspectives on children's self-control: The development of two rating scales. *Journal of Consulting and Clinical Psychology*, 50, 624–633.

Isoce, I. (1974). Community psychology and the competent community. *American Psychologist*, 29, 607–613.

Johnson, L. C. (1994). *Social Work Practice: A Generalist Approach*. (5th ed.). Needham Heights, MA: Allyn and Bacon.

Klein, W. C. (1992). Measuring caregiver attitude toward the provision of long-term care. *Journal of Social Service Research*, 16, 147–162.

Kovacs, M. (1981). Rating scales to assess depression in school-aged children. *Acta Paedopsychiatrica*, 46, 305–315.

Kral, R. (1995). *Strategies that Work: Techniques for Solutions in Schools*. Milwaukee, Brief Family Therapy Center.

Krumboltz, J. (1966). Behavioral counseling. *Journal of Counseling Psychology*, 13, 153–159.

Krumboltz, J. & Hosford, R. (1967). Behavioral counseling in the elementary school. *Elementary School Guidance and Counseling*, 1, 27–40.

Kurdek, L. A. & Berg, B. (1987). Children's Beliefs About Parental Divorce Scale: Psychometric characteristics and concurrent validity. *Journal of Consulting and Clinical Psychology*, 55, 712–718.

Laird, J. & Allen, J. A. (1983). Family theory and practice. In A. Rosenblatt & D. Walldfogel, (Eds.), *Handbook of clinical social work* (pp. 176–201). San Francisco: Jossey-Bass.

Leiberman, M. A., Yalom, I. D., & Miles, M. B. (1973). *Encounter Groups: First Facts*. New York: Basic Books.

Lindemann, E. (1944). Symptomatology and management of acute grief. In H. Parad (Ed.), *Crisis intervention: Selected readings*. New York: Family Service Association of America.

Lowman, J. (1980). Measurement of family affective structure. *Journal of Personality Assessment*, 44, 130–141.

Magura, A. & Moses, B. S. (1986). *Outcome measures for child welfare services: Theory and applications.* Washington, DC: Child Welfare League of America.

Magura, A., Moses, B. S., & Jones, M. A. (1987). *Assessing risk and measuring change in families: The family risk scales.* Washington, DC: Child Welfare League of America.

Mayer, J. & Filstead, W. J. (1979). The Adolescent Alcohol Involvement Scale: An instrument for measuring adolescents' use and mis-use of alcohol. *Journal of Studies in Alcohol,* 40, 291–300.

McCroskey, J., Nishimoto, R., & Subramanian, K. (1991). Assessment in family support programs: Initial reliability and validity testing of the Family Assessment Form. *Child Welfare,* 70(1), 19–33.

McCubbin, H. I. & Patterson, J. M. (1983). Stress: The family inventory of life events and changes. In E. E. Filsinger (Ed.), *Marriage and family assessment: A sourcebook for family therapy* (pp. 275–297). Beverly Hills: Sage.

Milner, J. S., Gold, R. G., Ayoub, C., & Jacewitz, M. M. (1984). Predictive validity of the Child Abuse Potential Inventory. *Journal of Consulting and Clinical Psychology,* 52, 879–884.

Minuchin, S. (1974). The Minuchin family stress models: A guide for assessing and treating the impact of marital disruption on children and families. *International Journal of Adolescence and Youth,* 1, 367–377.

Morris, L. W. & Engle, W. B. (1981). Assessing various coping strategies and their effects on test performance and anxiety. *Journal of Clinical Psychology,* 37, 165–171.

Mowrer, O. H. (1972). Integrity groups: Basic principles and objectives. *The Counseling Psychologist,* 3, 4–6.

Mullen, E. J. (1983). Personal practice models. In A. Rosenblatt & D. Waldfogel (Ed.), *Handbook of clinical social work.* (pp. 623-649). San Francisco: Jossey-Bass.

Nathan, P. & Harris, S. (1975). *Psychopathology and society.* New York: McGraw Hill Book Company.

Newbrough, J. R. (1971). Behavioral perspectives on psychosocial classification. *American Journal of Orthopsychiatry,* 42, 843–845.

Nowicki, S. & Strickland, B. R. (1973). A locus of control scale for children. *Journal of Consulting and Clinical Psychology,* 40, 148–154.

Olson, D. H. (1986). Circumplex Model Seven: Validation studies and FACES III. *Family Process,* 25, 337–351.

Olson, D. H. & Tiesel, J. W. (1993). Assessment of family functioning. In G. E. Hendershot and F. B. LeClere (Eds.), *Family health: From data to policy,* (76–97). Minneapolis, MN: National Council on Family Relations.

Pardeck, J. T. (1981). The current state and new direction of family therapy. *Family Therapy,* 8, 113–120.

Pardeck, J. T. (1982). Family policy: An ecological approach supporting family therapy treatment. *Family Therapy,* 9, 163–165.

Pardeck, J. T. (1989). Family therapy as a treatment approach to child abuse. *Family Therapy,* 16, 113–120.

Pardeck, J. T. (1993). *Using bibliotherapy in clinical practice: A guide to self-help books.* Westport: CT: Greenwood Press.

Pardeck, J. T. (1996). *Social work practice: An ecological approach.* Westport, CT: Auburn House.

Pardeck, J. T. & Yuen, F. K. O. (1997). A family health approach to social work practice. *Family Therapy*, 24(2), 115–128.

Pardeck, J. T. & Yuen, F. K. O. (Eds.) (1999). *Family Health: A holistic approach to social work practice.* Westport, CT: Auburn House.

Pardeck, J. T., Yuen, F. K. O., Daley, J., & Hawkins, C. (1998). Social work assessment and intervention through family health practice. *Family Therapy*, 25(1), 25–39.

Paulson, M., Afifi, A. A., Chaleff, A., Thomason, M. L., & Liu, V. Y. (1975). An MMPI scale for identifying "at risk" abusive parents. *Journal of Clinical Child Psychology*, 4, 22–24.

Payne, M. (1997). *Modern social work theory* (2nd ed.). Chicago: Lyceum.

Pearlin, L. & Schooler, C. (1978). The structure of coping. *Journal of Health and Social Behavior*, 19, 2–21.

Perlman, H. H. (1957). *Social casework: A problem-solving process.* Chicago: University of Chicago Press.

Plas, J. (1981). The psychologist in the school community: A liaison role. *School Psychology Review*, 10, 72Ä81.

Polansky, N. A., Chalmers, M. A., Buttenwieser, E., & Williams, D. (1978). Assessing adequacy of child caring: An urban scale. *Child Welfare*, 57, 439–449.

Polansky, N. A., Chalmers, M. A., Buttenwieser, E., & Williams, D. P. (1981). *Damaged parents: An anatomy of child neglect.* Chicago: University of Chicago Press.

Polansky, N. A., Gaudin, J. M., & Kilpatrick, A. C. (1992). The Maternal Characteristics Scale: A cross validation. *Child Welfare*, 71(3), 271–280.

Poresky, R. H. (1987). Environmental Assessment Index: Reliability, stability and validity of the long and short forms. *Educational and Psychological Measurements*, 47, 969–975.

Quay, H. C. (1977). Measuring dimensions of deviant behavior: The Behavior Problem Checklist. *Journal of Abnormal Child Psychology*, 5, 277–287.

Rahdert, E. R. (Ed.) (1991). *The adolescent assessment/referral system manual.* Washington, DC: United States Department of Health and Human Services.

Reid, W. (1978). *The task-centered system.* NY: Columbia University Press.

Reid, W. (1992). *Task strategies: An empirical approach to clinical social work.* New York: Columbia University Press.

Reid, W. (2002). Knowledge for direct social work practice: An analysis of trends. *Social Service Review*, (76)1, 6–33.

Reid, W. & Epstein, L. (1972). *Task-centered casework.* New York: Columbia University Press.

Rhodes, W. & James, P. (1978). *Emotionally disturbed and deviant children.* Englewood Cliffs, NJ: Prentice Hall.

Richmond, M. (1917). *Social Diagnosis*. New York: Russell Sage.

Roberts, A. (1991). *Contemporary perspectives on crisis intervention and prevention*. Englewood Cliff, NJ: Prentice-Hall.

Robinson, E. A. & Eyberg, S. M. (1981). The dyadic parent–child interaction coding system: Standardization and validation. *Journal of Counseling and Clinical Psychology*, 49, 245–250.

Rogers, C. (1970). *On encounter*. Harmondsworth, England: Penguin.

Rosenberg, M. (1979). *Conceiving the self*. New York: Basic Books.

Rothman, J. & Sager, J. S. (1998). *Case management: Integrating individual and community practice* (2nd ed.). Needham Height, MA: Allyn & Bacon.

Satir, V. (1967). *Conjoint Family Therapy*. Palo Alto, CA: Science and Behavior Books.

Skinner, B. F. (1953). *Science and human behavior*. New York: Macmillan.

Skinner, B. F. (1974). *About behaviorism*. New York: Knopf.

Snyder, D. K. (1983). Clinical and research applications of the Marital Satisfaction Inventory. In E. E. Filsinger (Ed.), *Marriage and family assessment: A sourcebook for family therapy* (pp. 169–198). Beverly Hills: Sage.

Snyder, W. & Ooms, T. (1992). *Empowering families, helping adolescents: Family-centered treatment of adolescents with alcohol, drug abuse, and mental health problems*. Office for Treatment Improvement. DHHS, Washington, D.C: U.S. Government Printing Office.

Spanier, G. B. & Filsinger, E. E. (1983). The Dyadic Adjustment Scale. In E. E. Filsinger (Ed.), *Marriage and family assessment: A sourcebook for family therapy* (pp. 155–168). Beverly Hills: Sage.

Stonebrink, S. (1988). *A measure of co-dependency and the impact of socio-cultural characteristics*. Unpublished master's thesis, University of Hawaii School of Social Work.

Straus, M. A. (1979). Measuring intrafamily conflict and violence: The Conflict Tactics (CT) Scales. *Journal of Marriage and the Family*, 41, 75–88.

Thompson, C. L. & Rudolph, L. B. (1992). *Counseling Children* (3rd ed.). Pacific Grove, CA: Brooks/Coles.

Toseland, R. W. & Rivas, R. F. (2001). *An introduction to group work practice* (4th ed.). Needham Heights, MA: Allyn and Bacon.

Turner, F. (Ed.) (1996). *Social work treatment: Interlocking theoretical approaches*. (4th ed.). New York: Free Press.

Turner, R. J., Frankel, B. G., & Levin, D. M. (1983). Social support: Conceptualization, measurement, and implications for mental health. *Research in Community Mental Health*, 3, 67–111.

Vaux, A., Riedel, S., & Stewart, D. (1987). Modes of social support: The Social Support Behaviors (SS-B) Scale. *American Journal of Community Psychology*, 15, 209–237.

Wahler, R. G., House, A. E., & Stambaugh, E. E. (1976). *Ecological assessment of child problem behavior*. New York: Pergamon Press.

Walsh, J. (2000). *Clinical case management with persons having mental illness: A relationship-based perspective*. Pacific Grove, CA: Brooks/Cole.

Warshay, L. H. (1975). *The current state of sociological theory*. New York: McKay.

Watson, G. (1967). Resistance to change. In G. Watson (Ed.), *Concepts for social change*. Washington, D.C.: National Training Laboratories, National Education Association.

Wodarski, J. S. (1981). *The role of research in clinical practice: A practical approach for the human services*. Baltimore: University Park Press.

Woods, M. & Hollis, F. (1990). *Casework: A psychosocial therapy* (4th ed.). New York: McGraw-Hill.

Yuen, F. K. O. (2005). Family health social work practice and change. In F. K. O. Yuen (Ed.), *Social work practice with children and families: A family health approach* (pp. 1–20). Binghamton, NY: Haworth Press.

Zastrow, C. (2001). *Social Work with Groups – Using the Class as a Group Leadership Laboratory*. (5th ed.), Pacific Grove, CA: Brooks/Cole.

Zatz, S. & Chassing, L. (1983). Cognitions of test-anxious children. *Journal of Consulting and Clinical Psychology*, 51, 526–534.

Chapter 3

A Call for Scientifically Based Practice

G reenwood (1957), a social work scholar, argued that the following attributes are critical for a field to possess to achieve full professional status:

1. A systematic body of theory
2. Professional authority
3. Community sanction
4. A regulative code of ethics
5. A professional culture.

After a critical analysis of the professional status of the field of social work in the 1950s, Greenwood (1957) concluded:

When we hold up social work against the model of the professions presented above, it does not take long to decide whether to classify it within the professional or nonprofessional occupations. Social work is already a profession; it has too many points of congruence with the model to be classifiable otherwise (p. 44).

Greenwood also noted that the power and privileges of a profession are extended to members through the acquisition of education designed to prepare practitioners for professional life (Meinert, Pardeck, and Kreuger, 2000). Even though Greenwood presents a firm argument for the professional status of social work, a number of critics have challenged his position (Pardeck, Chung, and Murphy, 1997). Collins (1975) offers other evidence that social work has not met the core criteria to be classified as a profession and that it remains at most a semi-profession. Collins suggests that this lack of professional status is largely due to the fact that social work continues to lack a systematic knowledge base that guides practitioners in a common approach to practice. Collins (1975) concludes that the field of social work lacks a clear theoretical base due to the tension found between social work and science, with science being referred to as a traditional epistemology grounded in an objective approach for discovering truth and developing knowledge (Meinert, Pardeck, and Kreuger, 2000).

SOCIAL WORK AND SOCIAL SCIENCE

There are a number of reasons that help to explain the tension between social work and science, which are signified by research activities on social work. One of the most common reasons practitioners offer is that research lacks relevance to direct practice. Many practitioners argue that research offers little to help with the day-to-day decisions made when working with clients.

Critics suggest that social work research follows a model grounded in the physical sciences that is mostly reductionistic. This model attempts to reduce phenomena to a limited number of independent variables for explaining client behavior. Even though this approach has been very successful in the physical sciences, it has limited utility for social work practice (Meinert, Pardeck, and Kreuger, 2000). They argue that science has not produced any widely accepted constructs about human behavior nor a sound theory for explaining the nature of human beings and why we behave as we do. Mace (1997) suggests that human beings are far more complex than phenomena found in the world of the physical sciences. Clients cannot be easily broken down into component parts that allow for scientific investigation. Given the complexity of human behavior, he concludes science offers little for improving social work practice.

WHAT'S ABOUT SCIENCE?

What is science? Science could be seen as a field of knowledge, a body of knowledge, or a state of knowing. It could also be seen as a way of knowing, a systematic and rational way of knowledge inquiry. Simply speaking, "Science (from *scientia*, Latin for "knowledge") refers to the systematic acquisition of new knowledge about nature and the body of already existing knowledge so gained. The scientific method is based on careful observation and the testing of theories by experiment" (retrieved from http://www.fact-index.com/s/sc/science_1.html on 08/10/04). There are rich histories of and debates over the utilities and limitations of science. Science and scientific approaches nevertheless have brought about much needed technological and social advancement in recent times. It is different from, as well as related to, other important human intellectual pursuits such as arts and humanities.

To further explore science, one has to consider the distinct differences as well as similarities in the nature, function, and approaches among the three main branches of natural science: physical, biological, and social science. Physical sciences such as physics, chemistry, and astronomy study the different aspects and events of the natural and physical world. Biological sciences such as biology, zoology, medicine, and dentistry study organisms, their evolution, and interactions. They are sciences of life. Social sciences such as sociology, economics, and psychology study the various dimensions and dynamics of our social and human world.

There are also differences between pure science and applied science. Pure science often grows out of curiosity and the desire to know. It seeks knowledge for knowledge's sake; but it also concerns the application of the knowledge gained. Applied science develops knowledge for practical purposes such as discovering an application, and inventing of knowledge to meet a need or to solve a problem.

One of the purposes of the application of science is to study, predict, and control. For example, it is through extensive studies that health officials predict the types and severity of the flu viruses for the upcoming flu season. Proper vaccination programs will then be in place to control and prevent a possible outbreak during the flu season. Not everything in the physical world can be studied and not every studied topic can help us to make accurate predictions.

Social work deals with the human and social aspect of our world. Controlled experimental or systemic studies are not the norm and often not feasible. Is it appropriate to apply strict physical science scientific approach standards to judge the quality of the social work profession? Should social work decide to become an art form or an academic discipline under humanities, then it may not need detailed discussion on its merits in science. Should social work decide to retain its claim as a social science profession, then the discussions would be on how and what roles scientific inquiry plays in the development of the profession. Many would agree that the practice of social work is both an art (a healing art) and a science. Science, therefore, is still a key component of social work practice. Hartman (1990) pointed out Clifford Geetz's (1983) assertion that "innovative thinkers in many fields are...finding art in science and science in art and social theory in all human creation and activity" (p. 4).

POSITIVISM VERSUS POSTMODERNISM

Fisher (1991) believes the field of social work has been grounded heavily in a postmodern epistemology since its founding. Meinert, Pardeck, and Kreuger (2000) view the strong influence of postmodernism as having resulted in a weak knowledge and theoretical base that seems to be interpreted and re-interpreted by each new generation of social work practitioners.

Positivism and postmodernism offer uniquely different views for knowing and understanding human behavior. Positivism has been the dominant epistemology in Western culture. Postmodernism has also been present in Western thinking; however, it has been clearly overshadowed by positivism (Meinert, Pardeck, and Kreuger, 2000). Table 3.1 provides the basic tenets for each approach to understanding the world and ultimately human behavior (Meinert, Pardeck, and Kreuger, 2000, p. 41).

It can be observed in Table 3.1 that the positivist versus the postmodern epistemologies present a much different view of the social world. The positivist approach suggests that reality is independent of the

Table 3.1 Positivism Versus Postmodernism Epistemologies

Positivism	Postmodernism
1. Reality exists independent of the person	1. Reality is constructed by the person
2. Absolute truth can be uncovered	2. Truths are relative to time and place
3. Knowledge consists of verifiable facts	3. Knowledge is a social construct
4. Meaning resides externally to symbols	4. Meaning is a result of social interaction
5. Knowing results from categorizing concepts	5. Knowing is an ongoing process of interpretation of events
6. Science is the core method for discovering truth	6. Science is an interpretative process unique to each observer
7. Causality can be discovered	7. Causality is a complex process involving numerous elements
8. Individual behavior is determinant and can be understood	8. Individual behavior is indeterminate

person; whereas the postmodern approach argues reality is created by individuals. The positivist worldview concludes truth is absolute; but truth is relative according to the postmodern approach. Knowledge development from the positivist's approach results from the categorizing of concepts; the postmodernist orientation views knowledge as fluid. The positivist views science as the core methodology of discovery; the postmodernist understands science as a process unique to the observer.

The profession of social work publicly endorses approaches grounded in the positivist's tradition to discovering new knowledge and theory building. Its strong reliance on "practice wisdom" as the dominant strategy for guiding practice suggests that the profession is also heavily influenced by the postmodern approach.

Given this tradition, Meinert, Pardeck, and Kreuger (2000) contend that social work practitioners continue to define and re-define themselves with each new fad that emerges in the popular literature. The result is a weak knowledge base that has limited grounding in sound social science theory. Under these conditions, theory development is often chaotic. Each collective of practitioners has its own unique idiosyncrasies in which it grounds its practice worldviews. These diverse types of practice wisdom would be helpful for formal knowledge development if they were to be properly organized, tested, and disseminated. Otherwise, this lack of knowledge boundaries within the field means social work knowledge development will continue to be short of focus and have problems finding a niche among the helping professions.

Scientific rigor is the goal of positivism. Meinert, Pardeck, and Kreuger (2000) propose that a sound knowledge base for social work practice will only emerge from a greater emphasis on science in the field of social work. What follows are brief histories of both positivism and postmodernism.

Positivism

The application of positivism emerged from the field of sociology in the nineteenth century. A number of social theorists, specifically French sociologists August Comte (1798–1857) and Emile Durkheim (1858–1917), viewed the social changes that occurred in the nineteenth century as a threat to the social and moral order of France (Aaron, 1968). Positivism was seen as a model that would offer strategies for dealing with the perceived breakdown of society. Aaron further explained the views of Comte and Durkheim as indicating that the spiritual and moral crises facing France could be resolved through positivism. They argued that positivism would provide the scientific based knowledge needed to replace social theories and philosophies largely built on speculation. The positivist model emphasized that knowledge should be based on facts derived from science. Positivism would provide a new episte-mology that would offer social order to societies on the verge of social chaos.

The social change that occurred in France in the late nineteenth century was largely due to industrialization, which brought growth and devel-opment, as well as a middle class that scoffed at tradition. Along with an increase in new wealth among the middle class, a proletarian class was also emerging. Durkheim concluded that these class divisions signaled the onset of anomie, a state of normlessness. Traditional values were disappearing and social order was breaking down. There were no clear social norms for people to follow.

A laissez-faire philosophy often associated with Scottish economist and philosopher Adam Smith (1723–1790) also took root in the nineteenth century (Aaron, 1968). The best society was viewed as one based on marketplace principles; thus the pursuit of individual economic gain was desirable and encouraged. Both Comte and Durkheim felt the laissez-faire philosophy had great limitations. They argued that a laissez-faire approach to organizing society created individuals who were so absorbed in their self-interests that traditional norms would gra-dually break down. The conclusion is that some norms could not survive without a universal set of values, when a mélange of competing claims would ultimately destroy the social order (Aaron, 1968). Positivism was seen as a scientific approach that would prevent such chaos.

Comte and Durkheim contended that knowledge and order are auton-omous, and thus these factors did not depend on individuals for their creation. This dualistic position concludes that facts and norms are thus categorically removed from the human experience. Positivism offered a logic that would result in a uniform knowledge base that could guide social development. Both theorists stressed that knowledge could be generated through the scientific model. As the logic of science was believed to be value-free, objective knowledge would be produced. Scientific facts, as described by Durkheim, are external and independent of the social world. Facts that exist external to the human mind are context-independent, and can be discovered through the scientific model. In this sense, Durkheim concluded that fact should be the truth and that it is synonymous with individual proclivities. He maintained that truth had to be impersonal and extra-individual. Understood this way, truth exists outside the social world and could be discovered through science.

Both Comte and Durkheim viewed society as similar to a living organism analogous to the human body. Similar to the organs of the human body, social institutions work in harmony with one another and perform functions that are critical to the survival of the whole system. Each component of the system is subordinate to the whole and guided by the telos that is assumed to be directing the operation of the body. Given this view, society is given primacy over the individual. "What is social," notes Durkheim (1983, p. 68), "always possesses a higher dignity than what is individual." That is, the individual's purpose is derived from the needs of the society.

European sociological theory greatly influenced the development of sociology in the United States, during what is called the period of early American sociology (1881–1930). Two themes emerged during this time. The first was an interest in making sociology a positive science. The second, organicism was revived in the form of a unique evolutionary theory that was underpinned by the notion that society could be improved through social engineering based on scientific principles.

Though early American sociology lacked sophistication, it still had considerable impact on modern day sociological theory. A more developed sociological theory of society emerged in the 1950s in Parsons' work. Parsons' application of systems theory of society was comprehensive and offered an objective approach to the study of society. Parsons' metaphor of social systems has had a tremendous influence on modern social work systems theory and practice. Similar to both Comte and Durkheim, Parsons too had a negative view of human behavior. Parsons believed that without some kind of external constraint, social chaos would result.

Parsons (1951) concluded that people could not be trusted to regulate themselves, because of their improvident character. He asserted that order would only prevail if individuals were structurally linked together. Parsons envisioned society as a system of specific roles that are in a state of "double contingency"(1951, p. 36). These roles were seen as linked through reciprocal obligations and sanctions. As opposed to volition, roles are united because of structural and functional necessity. The linkage between roles is thus guaranteed despite human involvement with the larger social world (Pardeck, Murphy, and Chung, 1994).

Unlike the positivist's view, postmodernism suggests that social cooperation can be achieved in a variety of ways. For example, individuals can reach a consensus through dialogue. This rendition of order, however, is predicated on the vision that persons are not atoms who are mostly self-consumed. But at least until the mid-1960s, most social theorists were not optimistic about this prospect. Wrong (1961) concluded that mainstream social theorists cling to an oversocialized concept of the person, whereby order is thought to be impossible without outside influences. Some type of autonomous apparatus, unadulterated by human bias and opinion, is required to secure order (Pardeck, Murphy, and Chung, 1994).

Postmodernism and Social Work Practice

Postmodernism celebrates diversity and suggests that reality is largely shaped by each person. There is no ultimate "objective reality." For example, being poor, homeless, an old person, or a person with a disability is largely defined by persons experiencing each of these personal situations; reality for each of these situations is defined by the person and shaped by other social systems such as a family, group, or organization (Fisher, 1991). Thus practitioners must be sensitive to clients' definitions to conduct appropriate assessments and interventions.

The disabilities civil rights movement serves as an example for illustrating the importance of enhancing practice and policy through the postmodern perspective. Science has been used for decades as the medium for defining the meaning of disability and this view has greatly influenced the larger society's perception that being disabled is found within the person (Pardeck, 1994). The disabilities civil rights movement has challenged this position and argued that the meaning of disability is found outside the self and is simply a social construction. This shift has resulted in empowerment of persons with disabilities and calls for a dramatic shift in how one conducts social work practice when dealing with persons with disabilities (Pardeck, Murphy, and Chung, 1994).

Practitioners argue that the postmodern perspective demystifies traditional theories and offers a new worldview. As suggested by postmodernism, accepted social scientific theories are seen as an extension of a dominant group's self-interests and its ideologies. The social realities experienced by oppressed groups are typically greatly different from those of the majority group.

A postmodern view suggests that there is no ultimate authoritative source of knowledge. For example, scientifically based research is treated with the same respect as other sources of knowledge. Knowledge is constructed through language and facts are embedded within language. Practitioners must be sensitive to these notions and to the necessity that social intervention must be "community based." Pardeck,

Murphy, and Chung, (1994, p. 114) summarize the core ideas critical to a postmodern perspective on social work.

1. Reality should be treated as socially constructed through language use. Norms, customs, and rituals, for example, are locally defined. Perelman's (1979) distinction between reasonable and rational behavior is useful at this juncture. His point is that no behavior is ultimately rational, but rather acts make sense only in terms of their social context. Practitioner judgments about normalcy or illness should reflect these various boundaries.

2. The methods used to gather information about clients should be attuned to the different language usages that are operative in society. Thus research instruments should be viewed as the means for engaging clients in dialogue. However, this is not the image of research that is usually presented. Instead, emphasis is typically placed on value freedom and maintaining a significant amount of distance from the client being assessed. This approach is thought to guarantee objectivity.

3. The interventions that are used should reflect, in Fish's (1980, p. 171) words, the "interpretive community" in question. What constitutes an appropriate intervention, successful treatment, or correct policy should be viewed as a local determination. The norms are defined by subjective experiences of community members, and could vary from community to community. A classic postmodern thinking of the Lebenswelt, the "lived world" of human consciousness, should be employed to guide intervention. As Ludwig Binswanger (1963) points out, a person's mode of being-in-the-world should dictate the need and course of treatment. Treatment should lead, in other words, and should not be prescribed by the requirements of an abstract social system.

4. The ethical principle that should guide treatment is to protect the integrity of a client's worldview. This position is different from that advanced by Parsons, for example, who maintained that the aim of intervention should be to restore harmony to social systems. As a result, the individual or community is sacrificed to the greater whole. Postmodernism argues that this abstract view is now defunct. The only exemplar that is available to ground an ethic is a patchwork of differences in the community. Suggested by this view is that the maintenance of these differences, as opposed to assimilation to an absolute ideal, should be the aim of treatment.

Finally, the general thrust of postmodernism has been to see social life as replete with possibilities. This linguistic social bond proposed by postmodernists is seen as more amenable to alteration and expansion than the standard structural version proposed by science. Fish (1989) is careful to indicate, nonetheless, that this rendition of social order does not immobilize persons and foster anarchy, due to an alleged absence of norms.

Norms are seen as local constructions that can be expanded. The point is that the choice is no longer between postmodernism or universal bases of social order. Through intersubjective activity, sometimes known as the realm of the "intertextual," order can be engendered (Pardeck, Murphy, and Chung, 1994). The message for practitioners is that social intervention is also an intersubjective endeavor that means treatment is a cooperative (relational) venture that is designed to protect personal or collective differences, thereby enlarging the social mosaic. This approach to treatment, according to postmodernists, is anarchistic only to those who labor to repair an ailing social system.

KNOWLEDGE DEVELOPMENT AND SOCIAL WORK PRACTICE

Both positivism and postmodernism have their merits and limitations for social work practice. The over reliance on one ideology over the other or the lack of congruency in the inclusion of both ideologies have had significant impacts on the knowledge development, academic status, and social acceptance of the social work profession. Meinert, Pardeck, and Kreuger (2000) believe that given the field of social work's alignment with postmodernism, it may place itself outside the mainstream of academic life. This positioning has resulted in questionable academic standards within the field of social work. The lack of commitment to science also ensures that the field of social work has limited status and influence within the academy. Furthermore, those disciplines that are more grounded in science, such as psychology, political science, and sociology, are well established within the university setting. Royse (2004) observed that "unlike psychology, which adopt the Scientist-Professional Training Model shortly after World War II, the dual emphasis on research and practice has not received the same emphasis in social work until fairly recent time" (p. 5).

Midgley (1999) asserts that social work has a checkered history in academic institutions and particularly in major research institutions. Social work is typically criticized by other disciplines because it does not emphasize scholarship and rigor. Midgley goes on to state that among professional programs, law and medicine are often seen as the more rigorous programs within the academic setting; social work most often is seen as the least. Meinert, Pardeck, and Kreuger (2000) believe that this status within the academy has negative consequences for the field of social work. As long as the field continues to reject the importance of science as the core modality for generating knowledge and rests its theoretical base on postmodernism and individual practice wisdom, the status of social work will continue to suffer.

An important factor that has contributed to this lack of status within the university is the lack of emphasis on the importance of the doctorate of social work degree. The lack of recognition of social work in higher education is worsened by the small number of doctoral graduates produced in social work each year. In 1964–1965, only 39 people received a doctorate in social work, by 1989–1990, the figure rose to 247 degrees received (Meinert, Pardeck, and Kreuger, 2000). Feldman (1999) cited Austin's (1998) findings that in 1981 there were 226 doctoral graduates. The number increased to 258 in 1996 and 297 in 1997. Feldman reported that "for the last two decades the yearly output of doctoral graduates in social work has remained below 300 and essentially stagnant (p. 179)." Feldman believed that the problem however is that "the rapid expansion of social work education programs has not been accompanied by a corresponding growth in the number of doctoral graduates to staff them (p. 179)."

Other disciplines produce much greater numbers of doctorate level graduates. For example, in 1990–1991, 5,272 doctorate degrees in engineering were granted, 2,238 doctorates in chemistry, and approximately 252 doctorates in social work. Graduate schools of social work are not graduating enough doctorate level educated social workers. This appears to have resulted in the field's limited abilities to commit to research, and to very little knowledge development based on the traditional scientific approaches.

Over a decade ago, Spaulding (1991) found that approximately 45 percent of faculty members in graduate level social work programs did not possess doctorate level education. Many of the faculty members were more grounded in their practice experience and might not have seen the priority of using science as the basis to knowledge development. Spaulding also found that only a small number of the recently graduated doctorate faculty in social work were exposed to the latest research methodologies. Green, Hutchinson, and Sar (1992) reported that nearly 50 percent of doctoral level graduates in social work did not publish in professional journals after receiving their degrees. This limited commitment to scholarship only contributes to the low status of social work within the academic community.

Jenson, Fraser, and Lewis (1991) found that many social work programs lack solid research foundations, which are essential for the efforts of scientific inquiry. For example, only one-fifth of the programs require one or more courses in statistics. Approximately half required only two research classes. This standard appears to have resulted in a large number of doctorate level social work graduates having poor preparation in the area of research. This lack of commitment to research at the doctorate level is even more obvious at the MSW level. Jenson et al. (1991) conclude:

Research training in social work is a prisoner of an out-dated paradigm. Focused largely on casework training at the MSW level, this paradigm insures that doctoral students will enter doctoral programs with weak research methods and statistics backgrounds. In the absence of greater vertical integration of research content, social work appears likely to remain a profession dependent, in large part, on other disciplines for knowledge generation. The fundamental structure of social work education must be reconsidered if the profession is to make a serious effort to generate its own research knowledge (p. 37).

Having doctoral level social work educators may increase the likelihood of having more emphasis on the use of research for social work practice and training. The reality of shortage of social work faculty has made some social work programs use more faculty whose terminal degree is MSW (Feldman, 1999; Zastrow and Bremner, 2004). Feldman (1999) expresses his concerns about this trend.

Instructors would lack advanced training in areas crucial to the future of the profession, such as application of state-of-the-art research methods for evaluating practice and programs . . . Such a solution would be likely to diminish the stature of social work and public support for it. Even more, it would widen the gap between practitioners' demands for research-based knowledge and the profession's capacity to generate it (p. 180).

This shortage could have some serious consequences for the field of social work and social work education. O'Neal (2000) reports in NASW News:

The prestige and influence of social work could erode as other professions do more and more research that has been historically done by social workers. Schools of social work would have to hire many faculty with their highest degrees in other disciplines, making them ill equipped to do social work research (retrieved 08/16/2004, http://www.socialworkers.org/pubs/news/2000/11/phd.htm).

O'Neal (2000) also reports comments by Ruth Dunkle, a steering committee member for Group for the Advancement of Doctoral Education that

"If we no longer have enough Ph.D. faculty, then we can't support the research efforts necessary to demonstrate that social work makes a difference" (Retrieved 08/16/2004, http://www.socialworkers.org/pubs/news/2000/11/phd.htm). Social work training would become technical school training such that graduates are only prepared to take orders and instructions from other trained professionals.

CSWE details its accreditation expectations for the research contents for BSW and MSW programs. The commitment and delivery of such contents however vary from program to program dependant upon the program's curriculum design and other factors. Variations also exist among doctoral programs. It is difficult to have a firm idea of the research capabilities of a graduate from a social work program regardless of the degree earned. Graduates need to know how to use research methodologies to produce professional knowledge and to inform their practice. It is vital for social work programs to prepare their students in developing their competency and appreciation for the use of scientific approaches in knowledge development.

The relationships between the apparent lack of commitment to science and the low scholarly productivity among doctoral level social workers and educators are areas that need further exploration. This is, however, not a recent concern. Abbott (1985) studied the research productivity pattern of 175 social work doctorates. She found that "graduates produce a limited amount of research" (p. 11) and "only an average of one refereed publication every other year" (p. 16). In fact, among the subjects, "thirty nine percent produced no refereed articles prior to 1976, and 46 percent produced no refereed publications in the later period" (p. 14).

What criteria are used to grant tenure and promotion when large numbers of social work faculty never publish? Meinert, Pardeck, and Kreuger (2000) indicate that if tenure and promotion are being granted based on non-scholarly performance criteria, then it becomes clear why social work has limited prestige within the academy. The lack of scholarly productivity among social work faculty does not promote the viability of social work within the larger society. It is extremely important that this situation be changed to enhance the survival of social work in the twenty-first century.

Kirk (1990) and Schilling (1990) report that many social workers do not rely on empirical findings as a basis to their practice. This finding is partially attributed to the poor research training social workers often receive at the graduate level. Many strategies have been suggested that might assist professional social workers to rely more heavily on empirical findings as the foundation for their practice. Pardeck (1991) proposes the publication of a clinical guide that outlines interventions that work. A number of fields, including medicine, have used this kind of approach (Meinert, Pardeck, and Kreuger, 2000).

The use of single-subject design had showed great promise for the profession; however, the enthusiasm for this technology quickly subsided. Brian (1990) concluded the following about empirical-based technologies such as the single-subject design:

That the empirical practice movement has had little impact on the profession at large other than social work education is not surprising for two reasons: one reason is that advocates of empirically based practice have made little effort to reach the profession at large, beyond publications and sessions at a few conferences. Second, many researchers have greater access to social work education than to organized social work (p. 6).

With this lack of commitment to empirically based practice, the field of social work will continue to use methods of intervention that lack efficacy. Until there is a greater commitment to empirically based scientific practice, the field of social work will have limited influence in the academy and among other helping professions (Meinert, Pardeck, and Kreuger, 2000).

SOCIAL WORK FACULTY AND SCHOLARLY ACTIVITY

Scholarly activity among social work faculty and practitioners is critical to the development of the field. The tradition of the practitioner-educator emphasizing practice involvement over scholarship no longer fits the realities of today's academic environment. Improving practice effectiveness and increasing scholarly publication should be two equally important considerations for social work practitioners and educators.

In the face of the university's standards calling for greater scholarly productivity, social work programs have begun to reconcile the tradition of practitioner-educator with the realities of today's academic milieu (McNeece, 1981). Social work educators are experiencing increased pressure to meet the expectations for scholarly publication. This is obviously difficult given the field's lack of commitment to scholarly productivity and science in general. As Euster and Weinbach (1986) note:

A social work faculty member may emerge from department, school, or college deliberations with strongly endorsed recommendation for tenure and/ or promotion and yet become bitterly disappointed where, at other levels of review, he/she may be judged as lacking in achievements expected of an academician (p. 79).

The denial of tenure or promotion of social work faculty due to their lack of accomplishment in scholarship not only affected the faculty but also the social work education processes. For example, Dinerman (1981) in her research on undergraduate and graduate social work programs found many undergraduate programs were staffed by large numbers of non-tenured faculty, especially faculty who lacked publications and doctorates. She concluded that the lack of tenured social work faculty raises concerns of program stability. In spite of her concerns, social work programs have been expanding tremendously in the past two decades. Pardeck (1991) contended that such programs may face an attitude of disparagement by academic colleagues and administrators who participate in resource allocation, and in tenure and promotion decisions. Even though traditionally social work faculty has not placed a strong emphasis on scholarship, university administrators and social work deans and directors have been found to highly value scholarship as a factor for tenure and promotion. With an increasing number of faculty members seeking tenure and promotion, the need for scholarly production would become more important. That is, research and scholarship as well as teaching performance, are receiving close scrutiny, focusing in particular on the quality and impact of an individual's work.

The lack of strong emphasis on publication of scholarly work is inconsistent with today's academic standards. The field of social work within an academic environment must behave and produce at the same levels of scholarship expected of other academic disciplines. The field's strong grounding in postmodernism needs to be supplemented by an even stronger engagement in science along with emphases on research and knowledge development to survive in the academic environment. At the same time, more attention should be paid toward the development and utilization of established postmodern research methodologies for practice research and scholarly publications.

GROUNDED SCIENTIFIC PRACTICE AND SOCIAL WORK

Accountability is more than a buzzword of the twenty-first century. It is a reality and standard for the social work profession. Within the clinical setting, clients are demanding proof that the goals and objectives of their treatment are being achieved. Funding agencies of social programs are placing greater pressure on agency personnel to prove their accountability (Yuen and Terao, 2003). This current trend can be partially traced to the Health Research Group, one of Ralph Nader's public citizens organizations (Adams and Orgel, 1975). In the 1970s the Health Research Group argued that people seeking help from human services professionals should demand a written contract that specifies the conditions of treatment, the goals and objectives of intervention, and the length of the proposed treatment. It also argued that the contract should specify the nature of the treatment including empirical evidence validating that treatment goals are being achieved. In recent years these principles have become standard protocol for most clinical interventions (Meinert, Pardeck, and Kreuger, 2000).

In the twenty-first century, the emphasis on accountability has emerged as a national policy aimed at improving human services and education. For example, in the area of education, the controversial 2002 *No Child Left Behind* national legislation mandates accountability of both state and local school districts in the education of children. These kinds of national and state mandates have also been applied in many social welfare programs.

The demands for accountability within the profession of social work and from clients are becoming louder and broader in scope. This trend is supported by the rising cost of malpractice insurance as well as courts ruling in favor of clients in an increasing number of lawsuits (Pardeck, 1991). There may be a worry that clients become upset by systematic evaluation of treatment procedures. However, no research data are available to support such a claim. In fact, Campbell (1988) concludes that clients are overwhelmingly in favor of systematic evaluation grounded in science and not simply the opinions of practitioners.

On the other hand, the demand for accountability provides social work faculty with a wealth of opportunities to begin meeting the expectations of scholarship within the academic environment. In essence, through scientific practice, social work faculty can achieve not only accountability in practice and treatment but also meet the demand for scholarship within the academic world.

The push for science-based practice is not a new idea. Scientific practice, sometimes referred to as "data-guided practice" or "practice research" (Thomas, 1977; Bloom, 1978; Pardeck and Murphy, 1986; Connaway and Gentry, 1988; Meinert, Pardeck, and Kreguer, 2000), has led many human services professionals to approach human services as a scientific discipline. For example, Jeger and Slotnick (1982) proposed a "behavioral ecological" approach to service delivery that is grounded in scientific methods and functions within the context of human ecology. Both the behavioral and ecological orientations have been well established in the field of social work. Together, they provide the foundation for the further development of scientific practice in social work.

Briar (1979) suggests that the practitioner within the academic setting can meet the emerging emphasis on scholarship by using empirical-based approaches, which include the following:

1. Use only methods of intervention known to have empirical validations;
2. Continuously evaluate treatment outcome;
3. Participate in the testing and reporting of effective practice techniques;
4. Use untested practice methods with caution and only with adequate control and evaluation of treatment outcome; and
5. Communicate the results of evaluation to other professionals (p. 132–133).

Conducting research in practice is clearly a mandate of the field of social work. The Council on Social Work Education (2003) calls for social work educators to understand and appreciate the necessity of the scientific approach to knowledge building and practice, including the scientific evaluation of practice. The National Association of Social Workers Code of Ethics that was approved in 1996 and revised in 1999 clearly concludes that scholarship and research are critical to practice and that practitioners must be guided by the conventions of scholarly inquiry. One must keep in mind, however, that these kinds of mandates from professional social work organizations do not necessarily mean practitioners are adopting scientifically based methods in the field as well as in social work education.

It is clear that a practitioner-educator in an academic setting must be committed to the production of scholarship not only because it is important for the field's development, but also because scientific inquiry is an essential part of practice and its advancement. Social work educators have an obligation to conduct research and to disseminate their findings through professional journals and other legitimate outlets such as national conferences. The quality of social work education will be positively affected by the influx of validated and proven knowledge and skills. The more important outcome will be the development of social work students who are prepared to become effective, accountable, and creditable practitioners.

Hudson's Scientific Axioms

An axiom is a principle assumption accepted as self-evidently true (Siporin, 1975). The following famous and controversial axioms have been developed by Hudson (1985, pp. 185–205) as a set of principles that can guide social work practice regardless of setting. They are grounded in the positivist's tradition and clearly reject the postmodern perspective. The following eight axioms move the practitioner out of the realm of theory and into the world of practical utility, where problems are assessed, measured, and treated (Pardeck, 1991):

"Axiom 1: If instruments are to have any practice utility they must have two fundamental characteristics: they must be valid, and they must be reliable" (Hudson, 1985, p. 185). The importance of this axiom is that regardless of the type of clinical instruments used by the practitioner, it is imperative that they have established reliability and validity.

"Axiom 2: In order for instruments to have maximum utility for social workers, they must be short, easy to administer, easy to understand, easy to score, and easy to interpret" (Hudson, 1985, p. 186). Many clinical instruments used in the behavioral or social sciences are long and complicated. They are difficult to interpret, score, or administer, and some are rather so technical that only persons specializing in psychometrics can successfully employ them in practice. Social workers should be trained to competently apply these instruments if they are appropriate for their practice. Practitioners should also develop instruments that are easy to score and interpret. Presently, there are numerous scientific instruments available for practice, which meet the criteria of Axiom 2.

"Axiom 3: There are only two ways to determine whether clients have problems: watch them, or ask them" (Hudson, 1985, p. 186). This axiom means that the practitioner can decide, on the basis of various observational approaches, whether a client has a problem in some area of functioning, or simply guide the client through various research strategies to report whether such a problem exists.

"Axiom 4: There are only four ways of measuring a client problem: in terms of its switch, frequency, magnitude, or duration" (Hudson, 1985, p. 187). If a problem is either present or absent this is referred to as a switch. This is a very basic but important measurement. Frequency refers to how often the problem occurs for the client. Magnitude measures the degree of presence or absence of a problem. For example, on a scale from 0 to 10, how serious is the depression the client feels? Zero may be coded as no depression present and 10 serious depression. Finally, duration is simply the length of time a problem has been present in a client's life.

"Axiom 5: If you cannot measure a client's problem it does not exist" (Hudson, 1985, p. 187).

"Axiom 6: If you cannot measure a client's problem you cannot treat it" (Hudson, 1985, p. 188).

"Axiom 7: If you cannot measure an intervention it does not exist" (Hudson, 1985, p. 188).

"Axiom 8: If you cannot measure an intervention you cannot administer it" (Hudson, 1985, p. 188).

The debates over the merits and the shortfalls of the above controversial axioms continue within the field. Some have focused on the spirit of these axioms that points to the need to use measurable concepts to formulate and implement various interventions. They also suggest the application of a logic model for problem solving. They identify the direct linkage between theory and how one can ground theory in social measurement. More importantly they offer a strategy by which the practitioner-educator can begin to think and behave in a scientific fashion. One of the key concerns here is "measurement." It involves operationalizing a variable into identifiable and assessable units. Measurement does not necessarily mean quantification of variables. It may also mean the identification of indicators that could reflect the state of the concept. Certain concepts such as "love" could not, and should not, be easily quantified and measured. However, one could find indicators that reflect the presence and the extent of such affection.

What should be stressed, however, is that practice activities must always be a major part of the social work educator's life. Scientific practice offers a strategy based in systemic inquiry, which allows the practitioner-educator to translate practice intervention into scholarship. The practical implication is that "scientific practice" presents a model for assessing and measuring intervention, which can be translated into sound scholarly production. Scientific practice could employ a variety of research designs or critical thinking approaches for assessing and measuring the performance of interventions. Social work faculty can be extremely creative in the application and development of such approaches and contribute to the professional literature. This process should address the need for increasing scholarly publication among social work educators, an expectation of all faculty regardless of discipline within the academic setting.

CONCLUSIONS AND IMPLICATIONS

In this chapter, it has been argued that the field of social work has limited commitment to rigorous scientific enquiry as its source of knowledge development. Even though the Council on Social Work Education (2003) accreditation guidelines identify research as an important curriculum content area, the empirical findings report that this curriculum area at all degree levels, the bachelors through the doctorate, is weak (Meinert, Pardeck, and Kreuger, 2000).

A sound knowledge base grounded in science has not emerged and there are not enough social workers involved in research and scholarly activity. Doctorate social work programs should be encouraged to put more emphasis on the application of rigorous research methods in the learning and development of social work knowledge. There are many reasons why MSW is the terminal degree for practice. However, MSW curricula simply do not enhance an appreciation for research or the importance of research and evaluation in testing practice and building theory. Given this situation, the field will continue to struggle because of its weak commitment to the development of its exclusive knowledge base—which means limited standing among other related helping professions and academic disciplines.

Social work needs to emphasize the use of scientific methodologies as the basic approach to knowledge development, even though some have suggested that science has little to offer practitioners. Science has much to offer social work practice and needs to play a central role in the knowledge development of the field.

Meinert, Pardeck, and Kreuger (2000) argue that social workers have mostly endorsed postmodernism, a perspective that challenges the traditions of positivism such as scientific practice. They believe that when ideology and individual reality are the only underpinning of a knowledge base and scientific rigor is suspect, knowledge development might have lost its relevance in the field of social work.

Finally, Lindsey (1999) reports the following consequences concerning the lack of commitment to research in the field as well as academic standards within schools of social work:

1. Cronyism and favoritism are found throughout the field in terms of academic appointments.
2. Many talented and gifted researchers have grown disillusioned and left the field of social work.
3. Social workers do not understand the importance of research in the development of knowledge and lack commitment to scholarly production.
4. The lack of research standards means the field is failing clients and may even become irrelevant in the twenty-first century (p. 119).

Social work educators must become more involved in scientific inquiry and scholarly production within the university setting. It is critical to the survival of the field of social work in the academy.

REFERENCES

Aaron, R. (1968). *Main currents in sociological thought I.* Garden City, NY: Doubleday.

Abbott, A. A. (1985). Research productivity patterns of social work doctorates. *Social Work Research and Abstracts,* 21, 11–17.

Adam, S. & Orgel, M. (1975). *Through the mental health maze: a consumer's guide to finding a psychotherapist.* Washington, D.C: Health Research Group, Public Citizen.

Austin, D. M. (1988). *A report on progress in the development of research resources in social work.* Washington, D.C: Institute for the Advancement of Social Work Research.

Binswanger, L. (1963). *Being-in-the-world.* New York: Basic Books.

Bloom, M. (1978). Challenges to helping professions and the response of scientific practice. *Social Service Review,* 52, 584–595.

Brian, S. (1990). Empiricism and clinical practice. In L. Videka-Sherman & W. J. Reid (Eds.), *Advances in clinical social work research* (pp. 1–7). Silver Springs, MD: National Association of Social Workers.

Briar, S. (1979). Incorporating research into education for clinical practice in social work: Toward a clinical science in social work. In A. Rubin & A. Rosenblatt, (Eds.), *Sourcebook on Research Utilization.* New York: Council on Social Work Education.

Campbell, J. (1988). Client acceptance of single-system evaluation procedures. *Social Work Research and Abstracts,* 24, 21–22.

Collins, R. (1975). *Conflict sociology: Toward an explanatory science.* New York: Academic Press.

Connaway, R. & Gentry, M. (1988). *Social work practice.* Englewood Cliffs, N.J: Prentice-Hall.

Council on Social Work Education (2003). *Handbook of accreditation standards and procedures.* (5th ed.). Alexandria, VA: CSWE.

Dinerman, M. (1981). *Social work curriculum at baccalaureate and masters level.* New York: The Lois and Samuel Silberman Fund.

Durkheim, E. (1983). *Pragmatism and sociology.* Cambridge, MA: Cambridge University Press.

Euster, G. & Weinbach, R. (1986). Deans' quality assessment of faculty publications for tenure/promotion decisions. *Journal of Social Work Education,* 22, 79–84.

Feldman, R. (1999). The human resource crisis in social work education. *Journal of Social Work Education,* 35(2), 178–181.

Fish, S. (1980). *Is there a text in this class* Cambridge, MA: Harvard University Press.

Fisher, D. D. V. (1991). *An introduction to constructivism for social workers.* New York: Praeger.

Geertz, C. (1983). Blurred genres. The reconfiguration of social thought. In *Local knowledge: Further essays in interpretive anthropology.* New York: Basic Books.

Green, R. G., Hutchinson, E. D., & Sar, B. K. (1992). Evaluating scholarly performance: The productivity of graduates of social work doctoral programs. *Social Service Review, 66,* 441–466.

Greenwood, E. (1957). Attributes of a profession. *Social Work, 2,* 45–55.

Hartman, A. (January 1990). Many ways of knowing (Editorial). *Social Work,* (35)1, 3–4.

Hudson, W. W. (1985). Indexes and scales. In R. M. Grinnell, (Ed.), *Social work research and evaluation.* (2nd ed.). (pp. 185–205). Itasca, IL: F.E. Peacock.

Jeger, A. M. & Slotnick, R. S. (1982). Community mental health: Toward a behavioral-ecological perspective. In A. M. Jeger & R. S. Slotnick (Eds.), *Community mental health and behavioral ecology.* New York: Plenum Press.

Jenson, J. M., Fraser, M. W., & Lewis, R. E. (1991). Research training in social work doctoral programs. *Arete, 16,* 23–38.

Kirk, S. A. (1990). Research utilization: The substructure of belief. In L. Videka-Sherman & W. J. Reid (Eds.), *Advances in clinical social work research* (pp. 233–250). Silver Springs, MD: National Association of Social Workers.

Lindsey, D. (1999). Ensuring standards in social work research. *Research on Social Work Practice, 9,* 115–120.

Mace, J. P. (1997). Introduction of chaos and complexity theory to social work. In D. J. Tucker, C. Garvin & R. Sarri (Eds.), *Integrating knowledge and practice* (pp. 149–158). Westport, CT: Praeger.

McNeece, C. (1981). Publication, tenure, and job satisfaction. *Journal of Social Work Education, 17,* 13–19.

Meinert, R., Pardeck, J. T., & Kreuger, L. (2000). *Social work: Seeking relevancy in the twenty-first century.* Binghamton, NY: The Haworth Press.

Midgley, J. (1999). Academics merit, professional needs, and social work education. *Research on Social Work Practice, 9,* 104–107.

National Association of Social Workers (1996). *Code of ethics.* Washington, D.C: Author.

O'Neal, J. V. (2000). Larger doctoral enrollments sought: Few social workers follow path to PhD. [Electronic version.] *NASW News,* November. Retrieved August 17, 2004 from http://www.socialworkers.org/pubs/news/2000/11/phd.htm

Pardeck, J. T. (1991). Using scientific practice increase scholarly activity among social work educators. *Education, 111,* 382–387.

Pardeck, J. T. (1994). *What you need to know about the Americans with disabilities act. Coping,* July/August, 16–17.

Pardeck, J. T. & Murphy, J. W. (1986). Technology and the therapeutic relationship. *Family Therapy* (Special Issue), 16.

Pardeck, J. T., Murphy, J. W., & Chung, W. S. (1994). Social work and postmodernism. *Social Work and Social Science Review*, 5(2), pp. 113–123.

Royse, D. (2004). Research methods in social work, (4th ed.). Pacific Grove, Brooks/Cole.

Schilling, R. F. (1990). Making research usable. In L. Videka-Sherman & W. J. Reid (Eds.), *Advances in clinical social work research* (pp. 256–260). Silver Springs, MD: National Association of Social Workers.

Siporin, M. (1975). *Introduction to social work practice*. New York: Macmillan.

Spaulding, E. C. (1991). *Statistics on social work education in the United States: 1990*. Alexandria, VA: Council on Social Work Education.

Thomas, E. J. (1977). The BESDAS model for effective practice. *Social Work Research and Abstracts*, 13, 12–16.

Wrong, D. (1961). The oversocialized conception of man in modern society. *American Sociological Review*, 26, 183–193.

Yuen, F. K. O. & Terao, K. (2003). *Practical grant writing and program evaluation*. Pacific Grove, CA: Brooks/Cole.

Zastrow, C. & Bremner, J. (2004). Research Notes: Social work education responds to the shortage of person with both a doctorate and a professional social work degree. *Journal of Social Work Education*, 40(2), 351–358.

Chapter 4

Professional Social Work Education

The Council on Social Work Education (CSWE) issued the first set of accreditation guidelines in 1952. The most recent guidelines for accrediting undergraduate and graduate social work programs were published in 2003 in the *Handbook of Accreditation Standards and Procedures*, 5th edition.

The *Handbook* (2003, p. 31) describes social work as a profession that promotes human well-being, by strengthening opportunities, resources, and capacities of people in their environments and by creating policies and services to correct conditions that limit human rights and the quality of life. Furthermore, the social work profession works to eliminate poverty, discrimination, and oppression. The social work practitioner is guided by a person-in-environment perspective and respects human diversity, and seeks to promote social and economic justice worldwide.

The *Handbook* concludes that social work education combines scientific inquiry with the teaching of professional skills to provide effective and ethical social work services. Social work educators reflect their identification with the profession through their teaching, scholarship, and service. Social work education employs educational, practice, scholarly, interprofessional, and service delivery models to orient and shape the profession's future in the context of expanding knowledge, changing technologies, and addresses complex human and social concerns.

CURRICULUM CONTENT AREAS

The undergraduate and graduate social work education is guided by eight curriculum content areas: Values and Ethics, Diversity, Populations at Risk and Social and Economic Justice, Human Behavior in the Social Environment, Social Welfare Policy and Services, Social Work Practice, Research, and Field Education. The following is the content covered under each of the eight curriculum areas (*Handbook*, 2003, pp. 34–36).

Values and Ethics   Social work education programs integrate content about values and principles of ethical decision making as presented in the National Association of Social Workers Code of Ethics. The educational experience provides students with the opportunity to be aware of personal values; develop, demonstrate, and promote the values of the profession; and analyze ethical dilemmas and the ways in which they affect practice, services, and clients.

Diversity   Social work programs integrate content that promotes understanding, affirmation, and respect for people from diverse backgrounds. The content emphasizes the interlocking and complex nature of culture and personal identity. It ensures that social services meet the needs of groups served and are culturally relevant. Programs educate students to recognize diversity within and between groups that may influence assessment, planning, intervention, and research. Students learn how to define, design, and implement strategies for effective practice with persons from diverse backgrounds.

Populations-at-Risk and Social and Economic Justice   Social work education programs integrate content on populations-at-risk, examining the factors that contribute to and constitute being at risk. Programs educate students to identify how group membership influences access to resources, and present content on the dynamics of such risk factors and responsive and productive strategies to redress them.

Programs integrate social and economic justice content grounded in an understanding of distributive justice, human and civil rights, and the global interconnections of oppression. Programs provide content related to implementing strategies to combat discrimination, oppression, and economic deprivation and to promote social and economic justice. Programs prepare students to advocate for nondiscriminatory social and economic systems.

Human Behavior and the Social Environment   Social work education programs provide content on the reciprocal relationships between human behavior and social environments. Content includes empirically based theories and knowledge that focus on the interactions between and among individuals, groups, societies, and economic systems. It includes theories and knowledge of biological, sociological, cultural, psychological, and spiritual development across the life span; the range of social systems in which people live (individual, family, group, organizational, and community); and the ways social systems promote or deter people in maintaining or achieving health and well-being.

Social Welfare Policy and Services Programs provide content about the history of social work, the history and current structures of social welfare services, and the role of policy in service delivery, social work practice, and attainment of individual and social well-being. Course content provides students with knowledge and skills to understand major policies that form the foundation of social welfare; analyze organizational, local, state, national, and international issues in social welfare policy and social service delivery; analyze and apply the results of policy research relevant to social service delivery; understand and demonstrate policy practice skills in regard to economic, political, and organizational systems, and use them to influence, formulate, and advocate for policy consistent with social work values; and identify financial, organizational, administrative, and planning processes required to deliver social services.

Social Work Practice Social work practice content is anchored in the purposes of the social work profession and focuses on strengths, capacities, and resources of client systems in relation to their broader environments. Students learn practice content that encompasses knowledge and skills to work with individuals, families, groups, organizations, and communities. This content includes engaging clients in an appropriate working relationship; identifying issues, problems, needs, resources, and assets; collecting and assessing information; and planning for service delivery. It includes using communication skills, supervision, and consultation. Practice content also includes identifying, analyzing, and implementing empirically based interventions designed to achieve client goals; applying empirical knowledge and technological advances; evaluating program outcomes and practice effectiveness; developing, analyzing, advocating, and providing leadership for policies and services; and promoting social and economic justice.

Research Qualitative and quantitative research content provides understanding of a scientific, analytic, and ethical approach to building knowledge for practice. The content prepares students to develop, use, and effectively communicate empirically based knowledge, including evidence-based interventions. Research knowledge is used by students to provide high-quality services; to initiate change; to improve practice, policy, and social service delivery; and to evaluate their own practice.

Field Education   Field education is an integral component of social work education anchored in the mission, goals, and educational level of the program. It occurs in settings that reinforce students' identification with the purposes, values, and ethics of the profession; fosters the integration of empirical and practice-based knowledge; and promotes the development of professional competence. Field education is systematically designed, supervised, coordinated, and evaluated on the basis of criteria by which students demonstrate the achievement of program objectives.

A successful social work program that integrates and delivers all these content areas should expect well-trained social work graduates who could perform effective and competent practice. Developing a program that meets the CSWE prescribed contents, local social service demands, and the sociocultural and political environments has been a challenge for social work programs.

Markward and Drolen (1999) criticize that the CSWE accreditation guidelines infringe upon academic freedom. If the content under a particular curriculum area is not covered—for example, qualitative research under the Research area—the program is at risk of not being in compliance with the CSWE accreditation standards. The accreditation standards by the CSWE may also have an effect on the choices of textbooks and instructional methods used by faculty members to cover all of the mandated curriculum content. In an attempt to standardize the teaching of a particular curriculum area or course content, or for other practical purposes, some social work programs may even dictate the textbooks used and teaching methods employed by faculty members: a policy that some would consider as infringement of faculty members' academic freedom.

On the other hand, one of the more obvious difficulties in the use of the curriculum standards is their vagueness. This vagueness may be intentional to allow flexibility in meeting individual program needs. Faculty has to first seek to understand the standards' interpretations of key terms and requirements, and then to see how a specific program is able to fit into those requirements. Otherwise, social work educators may have to take on the task of defending their own interpretations and applications of the standards. For example, under the curriculum area Populations-at-Risk and Social and Economic Justice, the term social justice has many meanings, and is often affected by one's political, academic, and other orientations. Liberals see social justice as an idea that is best implemented by government; conservatives would view such governmental involvements as oppressive. Furthermore, the standard does not define who is included under a populations-at-risk area.

Another concern of content area of research is the discrepancy between learning and application. Thus, content area emphasizes scientific approaches that include both qualitative and quantitative research methods. However, the literatures report that the use of empirically based research methods, both quantitative and qualitative, by social workers is rather minimal (Pardeck, 1991). Furthermore, it is illustrated in this book that social workers and educators do not aggressively use research as a method for developing knowledge. Given the reality of under-utilization of scientific methodology throughout the field of social work, the research requirements mandated by the CSWE are commendable efforts.

The CSWE curriculum standards have been criticized for being non-specific and often laced with ideology rather than concrete guidelines. The vagueness of the standards means social work faculty will have to decide for themselves what the standards mean to their programs. If the self-study document for accreditation or re-affirmation is done properly, a program could be in the position to implement a curriculum that reflects the uniqueness of that program. If not, a program may need to spend a considerable amount of its resources in understanding and shaping its curriculum to meet the CSWE criteria. Many have turned to experienced colleagues or paid accreditation consultants for assistance.

There is an inherent dilemma in the adoption of CSWE regulations. While it is necessary and desirable for the profession to standardize its training and its outcomes, that is, competent social work graduates, there is also the need to respect community demands and academic freedom in higher education. These seemingly conflictual demands in fact may be the two areas that the profession needs to elevate itself in to another level of professionalism and scholarly excellence. It takes both of them to complete the transformation of a sequence of course works into a quality professional education program that prepares competent social workers and meets the local needs.

SOCIAL WORK THEORIES AND PERSPECTIVES

There are a number of major theories and perspectives found throughout the social work curricula at the undergraduate and graduate levels. These include systems theory, the ecological perspective, and the generalist approach. The following offers an overview of these theories and approaches, particularly in relation to the family system.

Systems Theory

A system can be viewed as a whole comprised of individual parts. When change occurs in one part, the other parts of the system are affected. Systems theory focuses on linkages and relationships that connect individuals with each other such as those found in the family system. Systems theory provides a paradigm that focuses on multiple levels of phenomena simultaneously and emphasizes the interaction and transaction between parts. This theory helps social workers understand behavior in context and illustrates how systems impact individual social functioning. At a conceptual level, systems can be understood as open or closed. Healthy systems are typically open; closed systems are generally dysfunctional.

Open systems are those that exchange matter and energy with the surrounding environment. For example, a lighted candle that is covered with a glass jar is a closed system because the oxygen fuel supply is limited and, when exhausted, the candle goes out. When the glass jar is removed, the system is open to exchange gasses with the surrounding environment, constantly resupplying oxygen to sustain the burning candle.

The exchange process occurring between a system and its social environment is referred to as input and output. The resources used by a system to obtain its goals are the input. Likewise, output refers to the products created by systems after the input has been processed. Systems theory suggests that all systems attempt to maintain a steady state as they transact with their social environments. Furthermore, systems are self-regulating. There is a tendency for systems to seek equilibrium even when there are larger changes in the social ecology and at the end they will be affected. Through the input/output process, social workers realize the delicate balance between the client system and the larger community. For example, if a community could provide its families with quality educational as well as social and economic opportunities, these families will more likely be able to operate at an optimal level and contribute positive output in exchange. Lacking positive input from the community and meaningful interactions with its environments, a family system may gradually become a closed or imbalanced system. This dysfunctional system may be characterized by apathy or even abuse, neglect, and other kinds of depleting and non-productive behaviors. There is a positive correlation between the well-being of the community and its families.

Systems theory views communities as a critical human association that supports the family as well as other systems. These associations are based on ties of kinship, relationship, and shared experiences in which individuals voluntarily attempt to provide meaning to their lives, meet individual needs, and accomplish personal goals (Brueggermann, 1996). Communities are social systems that may take on various forms including churches and temples, ethnic and cultural organizations, neighborhoods, or families.

Another important concept in systems theory is equifinality, which means similar results can be obtained from different kinds of beginning points or means. "No matter where one begins with a system, the end will be the same" (Franklin and Jordan, 1999, p. 13). There are many ways to arrive at the same outcome. A person who is cold can get warmer by turning on the heater in the house or by just putting on more clothes. Similarly, one could use different routes and transportation to arrive at one's office from one's house. Different therapeutic interventions may use different activities but they all help to stabilize the family and to address its substance abuse problems. One of the responsibilities of the social worker is to help the client to identify possible alternatives, and select and implement the most desirable ones to achieve the set goals. On the other hand, multifinality (equipotentiality) refers to the potentials of starting from the same beginning or using the same interventions to arrive at different or multiple endings. The same event may have different effects on various family members and the same helping strategy may have dissimilar outcomes for different family members.

Nichols and Schwartz (1991) identified a number of basic tenets of systems theory that can be applied to social work practice with families. These tenets are important to practitioners using a systems approach to practice. They provide a holistic orientation to the assessment and treatment of the family system.

First, systems theory suggests that the whole is more than the sum of its parts. In relation to the family system, the family is more than just individual family members. The nature of the transaction and interaction between family members, the rules that govern these processes, and their repetitive patterns must be considered to gain insight into family functioning. Furthermore, the structural organization within the family is an important aspect of family functioning. Given the importance of the family system on the social functioning of the individual, it is an important target of social intervention in practice.

Second, a family systems approach places great emphasis on the contextual elements within the family system and the influence the larger society has on individual family members. These elements are often the target of family intervention at the micro, mezzo, and macro levels of interventions.

Third, the concept of homeostasis is critical to understanding the family system. The homeostatic process occurs when the family system responds to internal and environmental influences. Payne (1997) describes it as "the ability to maintain our fundamental nature, even though input changes us" (p. 138). Franklin and Jordan (1999) defines it as "a tendency of a system, such as a family, to try to maintain the system's equilibrium or status quo, even at the expense of making a positive change" (p. 428). Homeostasis enables a system to incorporate changes.

Fourth, the concept of circular causality offers an alternative view to the traditional models of understanding causality from a linear perspective. A systems approach stresses the reciprocal, interactional, and transactional pattern of behaviors that influence family functioning. Franklin and Jordan (1999) describe circular causality as "an idea from system theory which suggests that an individual's behavior is understood within the familial context, and one person's behavior is a reaction to and influences the behavior of others" (p. 83). Circular causality can be understood in a certain sense as a new epistemology in Western thought; however, it has been a dominant orientation of time and causality for many cultural groups. Kluckhohn and Strodtbeck (1961) and Nichols (1987) describe the predominantly spiral and present orientation of Hispanic and African populations and the mostly circular and past orientation of Asian populations which are in contrast to the linear sequential Western thinking. These time orientations are also related to the different beliefs that locus of causality is originated internally or externally.

Fifth, the family life cycle, is an important component of a systems approach to practice. Germain and Gitterman (1996) in their Life Model use the term "life course" to replace the traditional "life cycle." They refer life course as "the unique pathways of development that each human being takes—from conception and birth through old age—in varied environments and to our infinity varied life experiences . . . The term 'life cycle' is a misnomer, because human development is not cyclical . . . By contrast, the life course conception rests in an ecological view of non-uniform, indeterminable pathways of biopsychosocial development within diverse environments and cultures" (p. 21).

Systems theory provides a framework for social workers to develop an insight into understanding, assessing, and treating families. It clearly suggests that the individual is best understood within the context of the family system and individual functioning is connected to the functioning of the family system.

The Ecological Perspective

The ecological perspective stresses the reciprocal, transactional, and holistic dynamics that exist between the person and the environment. Germain and Gitterman (1987) identified the major concepts of the ecological perspective: reciprocal causality/exchange, adaptedness, life stress, coping, niche, habitat, and relatedness. The ecological perspective concludes that neither persons nor their environment can be fully understood except in relation to each other.

Ecological perspectives offer intervention strategies at multilevels such that social workers could impact client systems through macro level policy and planning activities as well as through therapeutic and other micro and mezzo level interventions. The ecological perspectives help social workers address problems and needs at various systemic levels including the individual, family, and larger community (Pardeck 1996). Meinert, Pardeck, and Kreuger (2001) summarized the key terms and concept of ecological perspective, discussed in Chapter 1 of this book. Pardeck and Yuen (1997) consider the family system to be one of the most important client systems that the practitioner works with. They identify six distinct professional roles that are found within the ecological approach to social work intervention (p. 124):

1. Conferee: Derived from the idea of conference, this role focuses on actions that are taken when the practitioner serves as the primary source of assistance to the client in problem solving.
2. Enabler: The enabler role focuses on actions taken when the practitioner structures, arranges, and manipulates events, interactions, and environmental variables to facilitate and enhance system functioning.
3. Broker: This role is defined as actions taken when the practitioner's objective is to link the consumer with goods and services or to control the quality of those goods and services.
4. Mediator: This role focuses on actions taken when the practitioner's objective is to reconcile opposing or disparate points of view and bring people together in united actions.
5. Advocate: This role is defined as actions taken when the practitioner secures services or resources on behalf of the client in the face of identified resistance or develops resources or services in cases where they are inadequate or nonexistent.
6. Guardian: The role of guardian is defined as actions taken when the practitioner performs a social control function or takes protective action when the client's competency level is deemed inadequate.

Often there are blurring and blending of roles in practice. For example, the roles of conferee and enabler are difficult to separate. When social workers implement the broker role, they may also find themselves enabling and advocating. The complementarities among the roles and their tendency to cluster rather than remain distinct should be noted. Social workers implementing the ecological perspectives are expected to have the knowledge and skills to work at multiple levels of the social ecology.

Generalist Social Work Practice

In searching for a "unifying conceptualization for the total profession," leaders in the field of social work have advocated that "generalist practice" is a useful framework (Landon, 1995, p. 1101). In Landon's review article on the generalist and advanced generalist models, she described the historical development of the models, indicating that by 1984 "generalist practice" was adopted by the CSWE as the standard for undergraduate social work education. She also acknowledged that "there is no agreed-upon definition of generalist practice, and CSWE has stated that all programs will proffer their own definitions and rationale" (1995, p. 1102). In fact, the primary commonalties she found were "the centrality of the multimethod and multilevel approaches, based on an eclectic choice of theory base and the necessity for incorporating the dual vision of the profession on private issues and social justice concerns" (1995, p. 1103).

Gibbs, Locke, and Lohmann (1990) describe two "central features" to the generalist practice model: "problem-solving centered rather than methods-driven" and "uses the person-in-environment configuration for assessment and intervention, giving practice a holistic emphasis throughout the entire problem-solving process" (pp. 234–235). However, they also acknowledge that "agreement on what is meant by 'generalist' and, in particular, 'advanced generalist' practice and education has remained problematic over the years" (p. 234).

Johnson (1995) describes generalist practice as consisting of the ability of the social worker to access at any level, and intervene with the appropriate skill, to assist the client system.

This is, in essence, the meaning of generalist practice. In developing a plan, the focal system for change may be any system experiencing a lack of need fulfillment or contributing to the lack of need fulfillment. The change strategy is chosen from a repertoire or group of strategies that the generalist worker possesses. This repertoire contains strategies appropriate for work with a variety of systems (individuals, families, small groups, agencies, and communities) (p. 13).

Kirst-Ashman and Hull (1997) emphasize the blend of knowledge, values, and skills to produce effective generalist results and offer the following definition of the generalist approach.

... the application of an eclectic knowledge base, professional values, and a wide range of skills to target any system size for change within the context of three primary processes. First, generalist practice involves working effectively within an organizational structure and doing so under supervision. Second, it requires the assumption of a wide range of professional roles. Third, generalist practice involves the application of critical thinking skills to the problem-solving process (pp. 7–8).

From the above examples alone, one can see the diversity of definitions of what a generalist approach is. Common themes include a multi-method, multilevel approach drawing from a vast repertoire of skills and including the ability to target any client system whether at micro, mezzo, or macro level. But the boundaries of what is not a generalist approach are not described. There are certainly themes of the can-do-spirit hidden in the generalist approach. Also hidden within the definition is the implied assumption that being non-generalist means being myopically capable in one method at one level, a professional preparation that few schools of any discipline would advocate.

Gibbs, Locke, and Lohmann (1990) also describe in their work the educational continuum from generalist to advanced generalist. They believe that since the CSWE revised the Curriculum Policy Statement in 1988 to acknowledge "advanced generalist" as one of the possible areas of specialty in graduate social work education, MSW programs have been "less consistent" than BSW programs in implementing generalist content into their curriculum. They found that social workers at both the BSW and MSW levels perform similar roles including: broker, advocate, evaluator, outreach worker, teacher, behavior change agent, consultant, caregiver, data manager, administrator, enabler, mediator, and community planner. What contrasts the generalist from the advanced generalist is "advanced generalist practice is defined less by the unique roles performed by MSWs than by the expectations of greater depth and breadth of performance . . . and the capacity for independent practice" (1990, p. 236). In other words, advanced generalist practice means more exposure to generalist principles in a more independent and complex practice setting.

Landon (1995) reported, "almost 100 percent of baccalaureate programs have a generalist core" as compared to a 1992 survey showing "55 percent" (11 of 22 programs responding) of MSW programs having an advanced generalist specialization (p. 1103). Further, all of the 11 programs, which had the advanced generalist approach, also had the generalist approach at the BSW level. Therefore the programs, which committed to the advanced generalist approach, had already embraced the generalist approach for their undergraduates. Advanced generalists are expected to apply generalist skills into "greater depth and in relation to more complex and technical issues" (Landon, p. 1105). In other words, the consensus was that advanced generalist practice was applying more developed generalist skills to more complex and difficult practice situations.

The advanced generalist approach is growing in popularity but is nebulously defined as an extra dose of generalist exposure. The demarcation line where generalist stops and advanced generalist starts is not clear. The MSW graduate theoretically has the same framework of skills as the undergraduate social work graduate. They just have more exposure to how the generalist model can be used in more complex settings. As generalists, social work students are trained to have skills and knowledge that can be used to impact multilevel systems. Advanced generalist practice increases the students' skills and knowledge in the areas of multilevel assessment and intervention. The practitioners at both the generalist and advanced generalist levels are expected to be able to apply critical thinking and to put knowledge to practice at the micro, mezzo, and macro levels.

The generalist model seeks to build a basic understanding of person-in-environment context for multilevel social work practice and the performance of different roles (e.g., enabler, advocate, change agent, administrator) to any setting where the social worker is employed. There is no central theory or focus. In fact, there is a strong emphasis on not having a central focus, rather to maximize flexibility and role definition. One may question whether the advanced generalist approach is like that of the emperor's new coat: everyone says it is there but no one can tell exactly what it is like. Another concern is that the advanced generalist would be at risk of becoming someone who is a "Jack of all trades, master of none."

STUDY FINDINGS ON SOCIAL WORK EDUCATION

Since the 1980s, one of the authors of this book (Pardeck) in particular has conducted a number of outcome studies measuring the effects of the social work curriculum in preparing students for practice. Although a good number of social work educators and practitioners are engaging in outcome and general research, the prevalence of the use and initiation of quality research projects among social work practitioners and educators s still lacking. Stoesz (1997) denounces and describes this situation in the following:

CSWE effectively condone flaccid research content. As inadequate research becomes normative for social work, the accreditation authority functions as nothing less than an "occupying army" of mediocrity. Not surprisingly, few graduate programs offer, let alone require, a research thesis. As a result, the research generated by MSWs in the field and published in the professional literature remains a novelty (p. 370).

Psychological Well-Being of Social Work Students

There is a speculation by some social work faculty that suggests social work students often are confronted with emotional problems (Cournoyer, 1983; Vodarski, Pippin, and Daniels, 1988) that may hinder their success as effective social workers. Pardeck and Chung (1995) conducted a small-scale study using a series of clinical scales measuring life satisfaction, self-esteem, and depression on a non-randomly selected group of undergraduate social work students. The total sample consisted of only 21 students. They found the students were all in the normal range on each of the clinical scales. Owing to the many limitations of this particular study, its finding could not be generalized to the social work student population. However, it is desirable for social work educators to further investigate ways to improve the well-being of social work students.

Gender Differences in Orientation to Clinical Practice

Weick (1994) questions whether women and men have a different orientation to clinical practice. Maher and Tereault (1994) argue that men and women have different worldviews due to personal experiences that are heavily influenced by their gender. Bensimon and Marshall (1997) further suggest that post-secondary education is a patriarchal organization that constrains equity policy and reproduces gender inequities between men and women professors and students, and the gendered consequences of neutral practices. According to feminist theorists, female clinicians should have a very different view of practice versus males and the academic establishment has not allowed this view to flourish.

Pardeck and Skibinski (1997) explore this argument through a randomly selected sample consisting of 28 males and 69 females who were MSW level licensed practitioners. Contradictory to the gender difference views, they found that men and women participating in their research did not have different worldviews toward practice. The two groups had very similar attitudes, philosophies, and behaviors toward clinical practice. In reality, most male and female social workers are self-selected groups who are attracted to the profession. As a result, they may have more in common or may be closer in many of their beliefs and philosophical orientations.

Beyond the discussions on the possible gender differences, the feminist perspective has great utilities for social work practice. Maher and Tetreault (1994) neatly summarize what the goal of social work education should be from a feminist perspective:

Feminist and laboratory pedagogies aimed to encourage the students, particularly women, working-class students, and members of underrepresented ethnic groups, to gain an education that would be relevant to their concerns, to create their own meanings, and to find their own voices in relation to the material. Just as the constructivist forms of knowledge are based on the experiences and viewpoints of all groups in society and not just the most powerful, so does the enactment of these new epistemologies in the classroom draw upon the viewpoints and experiences of students and teachers in new ways (p. 9).

The Impact of the Social Work Curriculum on Parenting and Child Development

Pardeck, Chung, Nielson, and Stokes (1991) reported that the undergraduate social work curriculum does not have any clear impact on changing attitudes toward parenting and child development. In this research, 104 undergraduate social work students were surveyed with an adult-adolescent parenting inventory. The inventory measured attitudes about child development, children's needs, the use of corporal punishment, and parenting roles. Students completing the inventory at the beginning and end of the social work program had very similar scores on the inventory.

The Impact of a Diversity Course on Social Work Students

Yuen and Pardeck (1998) examined the impact of a human diversity course on undergraduate social work students. A total of 153 students who were taught by the same instructor for the same undergraduate human diversity course over a three-year time period participated in this pre-post survey study. The findings suggested that the course had a positive impact on the students' attitudes toward diversity. However, what the study did note is that there are certain characteristics that may contribute to a more productive class experience. They include students being able to participate and to discuss freely in the course, insuring that one group is not presented as being superior to another, and making efforts to affirm that students of any background are not automatically made to feel guilty about the experiences of people of another group. Lack of these characteristics may even generate unspoken resentment toward certain groups. This study affirms the values of the diversity content of social work education but also highlights the importance of instilling an open and receptive classroom environment for the exchange of diverse ideas and opinions.

Personal Growth and Development and Undergraduate Social Work Education

According to Johnson (1972), the social work graduate should possess the following characteristics upon graduation:

1. Have a generally positive view of persons and their behavior.
2. Be concerned about others and their well-being for the sake of the others, not for self-centered purposes.
3. Be open, trusting, warm, friendly, and honest.
4. Work with persons being helped, not for them.
5. Respond to people rather than support the use of a particular technique.
6. Be mature, have good judgment, and be willing to take risks in the service to others.

For students to achieve the above characteristics, social work education should teach appropriate social work values, knowledge, and skills that enhance these characteristics as well as the students' personal growth and development.

Pardeck and McCallister (1991) explored the impact of undergraduate social work education on students' growth and development through a sample consisting of 78 students. The students represented two different social work programs. One program totaled 38 students participating in the study; the other program had 40 student participants. The students were divided into two groups within each program, beginning and graduating students.

Personal growth and development was measured through three different scales; College Self-Expression Scale (Galiassi et al., 1974), Generalized Contentment Scale (Hudson, 1982), and the Self-Esteem Scale

Table 4.1 Mean scores on the college self-expression scale, generalized contentment scale, and the self-esteem scale for beginning and graduating students

	Mean	N	SD	F
College Self-Expression Scale				
Midsouthern Program				
Beginning Students	122.35	23	18.28	0.58 NS
Graduating Students	122.33	15	23.37	
Midwestern Program				
Beginning Students	110.47	19	10.47	2.00 NS
Graduating Students	117.47	21	14.81	
Generalized Contentment Scale				
Midsouthern Program				
Beginning Students	26.26	23	10.43	1.24 NS
Graduating Students	22.53	15	12.11	
Midwestern Program				
Beginning Students	31.89	19	12.28	1.64 NS
Graduating Students	25.14	21	15.72	
Self-Esteem Scale				
Midsouthern Program				
Beginning Students	25.57	23	12.81	1.12 NS
Graduating Students	23.55	15	14.77	
Midwestern Program				
Beginning Students	37.42	19	17.86	1.25 NS
Graduating Students	27	21	15.96	

NS=Not statistically significant

(Hudson, 1982). As can be observed in Table 4.1, there were no statistically significant differences on any of the three measures used for beginning and graduating students. The extent of student growth and development in the undergraduate programs were unclear.

Degreed and Non-degreed Licensed Social Workers

Virtually all states now regulate social work practice through some form of licensure or certification. As the passage of a licensure bill is a highly political process, some states had to have a "grandfathering" clause to insure a bill's passage. Grandfathering a person for licensure usually means the person has practice experience but does not possess a professional degree in social work.

Pardeck, Chung, and Murphy (1997) explored how those who received a social work licensure without an MSW degree versus those licensed with the MSW degree differed in their attitudes and behaviors, philosophies, and political beliefs about practice. This study did not investigate the effectiveness or outcomes of the participants' clinical practice. This study, however, has important implications for the impact that the social work curriculum has on preparing students for practice.

The study included 155 randomly selected respondents who obtained a clinical license with or without the MSW degree. Ninety-seven of the respondents obtained a license with an MSW degree; 58 obtained a license without the MSW degree. The researchers found virtually no significant differences between the two groups in their attitudes and behaviors toward practice or their philosophical and political beliefs about practice.

Tables 4.2 and 4.3 report the findings for the practice modalities used by the two groups and their attitudes and behaviors. The study findings revealed there were no statistically significant differences between the groups in the practice modalities used. Furthermore, systems theory was the dominant modality most often used by both groups. These findings suggest that the practice experience used by the non-MSW degree respondents to obtain a license appeared to equal the formal social work education of the MSW respondents in terms of preparation for practice. These findings may raise the question of whether the formal social work education process is unique and necessary. If the answer is in the affirmative, social work education may leave much to be desired as practice experience appears to be as effective as formal social work education in

Table 4.2 Practice modalities used in practice

Modalities used in practice	Licensed With MSW ($n = 96$)		Licensed Without MSW ($n = 57$)		X2
	Yes (%)	No (%)	Yes (%)	No (%)	
Behavior therapy	8	92	18	82	2.92 NS
Psychodynamic therapy	19	81	18	92	0.04 NS
Systems theory	33	67	28	72	0.46 NS
Humanistic therapy	6	94	14	86	2.61 NS
Cognitive therapy	23	77	19	81	0.28 NS

NS=Not statistically significant

Table 4.3 MSWs and non MSWs attitudes and behaviors toward practice

	Licensed With MSW ($n = 93$)	Licensed Without MSW ($n = 52$)	
	Mean Score	Mean Score	F Score
1. Your treatment focus is on the individual and changing his/her personality/behavior	2.76	2.5	0.53 NS
2. Your treatment focus includes changing the client's/patient's social situation (employment, family, community, etc.)	2.1	2.3	1.72 NS
3. It is important to work with culturally diverse populations of clients/patients	1.9	2.0	0.74 NS
4. It is important to help the economically disadvantaged as part of one's practice	1.7	1.7	0.06 NS
5. It is important to be politically active to promote social change as part of one's practice	2.3	2.3	0.05 NS
6. It is important to be involved in professional organizations	1.92	2.2	0.78 NS

NS=Not statistically significant

preparing clinicians for practice. Certainly, there are many unanswered questions and variables that should be considered. What academic preparations or on-the-job training do these non-MSWs have? How many years of social work related experience have they had? Will the findings be the same if the targeted populations are non-clinical social workers?

CONCLUSIONS AND IMPLICATIONS

Social work programs accredited by the CSWE educate students for practice at the entry and advanced levels. Within this context, the following are a few additional considerations for social work programs in their preparation of graduates to become effective practitioners in the field:

1. Further examine whether social work curricula are more grounded in ideology than on scientifically based evidence. Students need to be exposed to curriculum content that is not only guided by ideology and philosophy but also grounded in scientific evidence.

2. Social work programs need to empirically evaluate the effectiveness of their curricula to ensure students are competently prepared for practice.
3. Most materials offered in social work curricula are borrowed from other disciplines. It is imperative that social work faculty and the field in general develop knowledge and skills unique to the field of social work. The development and ownership of an exclusive knowledge base signifies the professionalism of social work practice.
4. There is still a lack of evidence to suggest that graduates of social work programs experience personal growth and development as a result of their education. Social work programs may need to further examine whether such growth and development have been achieved and how best to make them attainable.

This chapter reviews social work education in the United States. While much has been accomplished, much more needs to be done. Critical self-evaluation and questioning the obvious contributes to professional growth; social work educators may wish to continuously question the effectiveness and appropriateness of our discipline's professional and educational approaches.

REFERENCES

Bensimon, E. M. & Marshall, C. (1997). Policy analysis for postsecondary education. In C. Marshall (Ed.), *Feminist critical policy analysis II: A perspective from postsecondary education*. Washington, DC: Falmer.

Brueggermann, W. (1996). *The practice of macro social work*. Chicago, IL: Nelson Hall.

Council on Social Work Education, (2003). *Handbook of Accreditation Standards and Procedures* (5th ed). Washington, DC: *Author*.

Cournoyer, B. (1983). Assertiveness among MSW students. *Journal of Social Work Education*, 19, 2430.

Franklin, C. & Jordan, C. (1999). *Family practice: Brief systems methods for social workers*. Pacific Grove, CA: Brooks/Cole.

Galiassi, J., Delo, J., Galiassi, M., & Bastien, S. (1974). The college self-expression scale: A measure of assertiveness. *Behavior Therapy*, 5, 165–171.

Germain, C. B. & Gitterman, A. (1987). Ecological perspective. In A. Minahan (Ed.), *Encyclopedia of social work* (18th ed.), pp. 488–499. Silver Spring, MD: NASW.

Germain, C. B. & Gitterman, A. (1996). *The life model of social work practice: Advances in theory & practice* (2nd ed.). New York: Columbia University Press.

Gibbs, P., Locke, B., & Lohmann, R. (1990). Paradigm for the generalist, advanced generalist continuum. *Journal of Social Work Education*, 3, 232–243.

Hudson, Walter W. (1982). *The clinical measurement package: A field manual*. Homewood, Ill: Dorsey Press.

Johnson, D. (1972). *Reaching out: Interpersonal effectiveness and self-actualization*. Englewood Cliffs, NJ: Prentice-Hall.

Johnson, L. C. (1995). *Social work practice: A generalist approach* (5th ed.). Boston, MA: Allyn and Bacon.

Kirst-Ashman, K. K. & Hull, G. H. (1997). *Generalist practice with organizations and communities*. Chicago, IL: Nelson Hall.

Kluckhohn, F. & Strodtbeck, F. (1961). *Variations in value orientations*. Evanston, IL: Row, Peterson.

Landon, P. S. (1995). Generalist and advanced generalist practice. In R. L. Edwards (Ed.), *Encyclopedia of social work* (19th ed.), pp. 1101–1108. Washington, DC: NASW Press.

Maher, F. & Tereault, M. K. T. (1994). *The feminist classroom*. New York: HarperCollins.

Markward, M. & Drolen, C. S. (1999). Do accreditation requirements deter curriculum innovation? *Journal of Social Work Education*, 35, (2), 183–112.

Meinert, R., Pardeck, J. T., & Kreuger, L. (2000). *Social work: Seeking relevancy in the twenty-first century*. Binghamton, NY: The Haworth Press.

Nichols, E. (1987). *The philosophical aspects of cultural differences*. Presented at the First Annual National Association of Social Work. Conference, New Orleans, LA.

Nichols, M. P. & Schwartz, R. C. (1991). *Family therapy: Concepts and methods* (2nd ed.). Needham Heights, MA: Allyn and Bacon.

Paradeck, J. T. (1991). Using scientific practice increases scholarly activity among social work educators. *Education*, III, 382–387.

Pardeck, J. T. (1996). *Social work practice: An ecological approach*. Westport, CT: Auburn House.

Pardeck, J. T. & Chung, W. S. (1995). An empirical analysis of the psychological well-being of undergraduate students in social work. *Family Therapy*, 22, 121–124.

Pardeck, J. T., Chung, W. S. & Murphy, J. W. (1995). An examination of the scholarly productivity of social work journal editorial board members and guest reviewers. *Research on Social work Practice*, 5, 223–234.

Pardeck, J. T., Chung, W. S., & Murphy, J. W. (1997). Degreed and nondegreed licensed clinical social workers: an exploratory study. *Journal of Sociology and Social Welfare*, 24(2), 143–178.

Pardeck, J. T., Chung, W. S., Nielson, J. & Stokes, J. L. (1991). An analysis of the impact of social work curriculum on the attitudes of students toward parenting and child development. *Family Therapy*, 18(3), 241–244.

Pardeck, J. T. & McCallister, A. (1991). The effects of undergraduate social work education on the personal growth and development of students. *Education*, 112, 382–387.

Pardeck, J. T. & Skibinski, G. J. (1997). An exploratory study of sex differences in orientation to clinical practice. *Psychological Reports*, 81, 1392–1394.

Pardeck, J. T. & Yuen, F. K. O. (1997). A family health approach to social work practice. *Family Therapy*, 24(2), 115–128.

Payne, M. (1997). *Modern social work theory*. (2nd ed.) Chicago, IL: Lyceum.

Reisch, M. & Gambrill, E. (Eds.) (1997). *Social work in the 21st century*. Thousand Oaks, CA: Sage.

Schatz, M., Jenkins, L., & Sheafor, B. (1990). Milford redefined: A model of initial and advanced generalist social work. *Journal of Social Work Education*, 26(3), 217–231.

Stoesz, D. (1997). The end of social work. In M. Reisch & Gambrill, E. (Eds.), *Social Work in the 21st century*. (368–375). Thousand Oaks, CA: Sage.

Weick, A. (1994). Overturning oppression: An analysis of emancipatory change. In L. Davis (Ed.), *Building on women's Strengths: A Social work agenda for the 21st century*. pp. 211–228. Binghamton, NY: Haworth.

Wodarski, J., Pippin, J., & Daniels, M. (1988). The effects of graduate social work education on personality, values, and interpersonal skills. *Journal of Social Work Education*, 24, 266–277.

Yuen, F. K. O. & Pardeck, J. T. (1998). Impact of human diversity education on social work students. *International Journal of Adolescence & Youth*, 17(3), 249–261.

Chapter 5

Scholarly Productivity of Social Work Journal Reviewers

The development of the field of social work has had many challenges and successes. This chapter uses the scholarly productivity of journal editors as an example to point out the urgency and need for the field to fiercely engage in the use of scientific approaches to empirically establish its knowledge base and credibility. As a practice profession, its core concern is the efficiency and effectiveness of its interventions and performance. However, the development of the profession's knowledge base is the prerequisite for such success in practice. It is through this critical and rigorous self-assessment and improvement that the missions of the profession could be successfully achieved.

Peer reviewed professional and academic journals are vital to the development of new knowledge within academic disciplines. The editorial boards of journals play a critical role in deciding what articles will be published for public dissemination. In the field of social work, since the 1970s, a number of studies have been conducted exploring the scholarly productivity of social work editorial boards, journal guest editorials, and journal editors. Many of the various reviewers found that most social work journals studied fell short in the area of scholarly productivity. This circumstance raises serious concerns about the fairness and quality of the articles published in the journals of this field. What follows is a review of the studies conducted on this important topic of scholarly productivity.

REVIEW OF THE RESEARCH ON THE SCHOLARLY PRODUCTIVITY OF SOCIAL WORK JOURNAL REVIEWERS

In the 1970s, Lindsey (1976, 1977a,b, 1978a,b) found that social work editorial boards, when compared to editorial boards in disciplines such as psychology and sociology, often lack distinction and achievement in the area of scholarly productivity. Lindsey measured scholarly productivity by the number of articles that members of editorial boards had published and how often they were cited by others in the literature. What was particularly fascinating about the research conducted by Lindsey was that social work journals would not publish his work. Lindsey concluded (1978a):

The most obvious finding is that the social work editorial boards are consistently composed of individuals who, in comparison to the editors of sociology and psychology, are not distinguished by the excellence or volume of their own contributions to the knowledge base of the field (p. 42).

Epstein (1990a,b) was another researcher who published a serious analysis of social work editorial boards. Epstein sent two versions of a previously published article to selected social work journals for review; the difference being that one version presented a positive impact of social work intervention while the other presented a negative outcome of social work treatment. Epstein was attempting to find if social work journals had a tendency to publish only articles that supported the effectiveness of social work intervention. Epstein found that the 53 social work journals that reviewed the two versions of the article had a tendency to reject the one that had findings with a negative outcome of social work intervention and to accept for publication the version with a positive treatment outcome. What struck Epstein about the review process was the poor quality of the reviews by the social work editorial board members. Epstein (1990a) concluded:

Except for the single review just noted every other review from a journal edited in a social work setting was flawed as an objective scientific critique. The reviewers were not knowledgeable in the subject area; they lacked minimal methodological sophistication; and they frequently intruded subjective, personal, or otherwise ideological opinions into their evaluations (p. 23).

Epstein (1992) succinctly summarized the state of social work editorial boards and the field in general in the following terms:

Social workers on editorial boards are drawn out of the undistinguished base of social work academics. Large numbers of tenured professors, even in prominent schools of social work, have never published anything. For others, productivity halted after being awarded tenure. Many appointments to social work faculties have little to do with teaching, scholarly, or intellectual competence. They seem to have a lot to do with the traditional varieties of corruption (nepotism, cronyism, trading favors, and the fecundity of incompetent selection committees in replicating themselves) and their New Age variants (compensatory appointments on the basis of gender, race, sexual preference, and ethnicity and political correctness). An undergraduate degree in social work today does not certify literacy. A graduate degree does not certify competence. An appointment to a social work faculty does not certify merit (p. 527).

Like Lindsey, Epstein found it was impossible to publish his study in a social work journal. Epstein's (1990a) findings appeared in an interdisciplinary journal entitled *Science, Technology, & Human Values*. Epstein (1990b) also found that the reporting of these findings resulted in his work and research methods being investigated by the National Committee on Inquiry of the National Association of Social Workers (NASW). Epstein (1990b) concluded:

If its qualitative analysis had been summed up as a whispered reminder that social work referees might profit from greater attention to their comments; if its quantitative analysis had been simply reported as disconfirmatory; then perhaps little would have been made of the paper. Even assuming that a charge would have been brought, the National Committee on Inquiry of the National Association of Social Workers might have accepted the research with more collegial regard. As it was, the National Committee sought to banish me from social work (p. 244).

It should be noted that the methodology employed by Epstein (1990a): submitting a contrived research paper to journals and subsequently evaluating the journal manuscript review process, raised critical ethical questions that were the focus of the NASW inquiry. For example, informed consent was not obtained from the unwitting participants in the study (i.e., the manuscript reviewers and journal editors). However, similar methodologies have been employed by researchers in other disciplines (e.g., Mahoney, 1977; Peters and Ceci, 1982) and appear to be a legitimate method of conducting such analyses. Epstein was eventually exonerated of violating the NASW Code of Ethics (Epstein, 1992).

The poor quality of social work editorial boards has resulted in other disciplines paying virtually no attention to the social work literature. Cheung (1990) found that social work journals cited psychiatry, sociology, and family studies journals 4.7, 5.4, and 2.3 times more often between 1981 and 1985 than they were in turn cited by journals in these respective fields. Epstein (1992) also concluded that the impact of social work journals is astoundingly low. For example, the Social Science Citation Index in 1989 reports that *Social Work* and *Social Services Review* had impact ratings of 0.73 and 0.45; these two journals are arguably the most prestigious journals in the field. These scores are far below the impact ratings of major journals in psychology, political science, and sociology.

Fraser and others (1991) found that the extent of research papers published in social work journals was poor. They viewed fifteen social work journals between 1985 and 1988 and discovered few articles that used systematic data collection technologies. The use of the experimental design was nonexistent in the journals. Most findings in the journals studied relied on rudimentary descriptive or univariate research approaches. The poor quality of research found in the social work journals may reflect inadequacies both in the research education of graduate schools of social work and in the evaluation process of articles. Fraser and others (1991) concluded from their research that more doctoral level social workers need to be produced and that there needs to be greater emphasis on science in all aspects of the social work curriculum. They further contended that the quality of published research in social work journals will continue to suffer unless more emphasis is placed on research in the field of social work. Meinert, Pardeck, and Krueger (2000) believe the status of social work within the university community could increase if the profession begins to adhere to the canons of science as the basis for knowledge development.

Building on the methodology established by Duncan Lindsey, Pardeck (1992) selected five prominent social work journals and five leading psychology journals and compiled a list of their editorial board members: 165 psychologists and 69 social workers. Using the *Social Sciences Citation Index* database, Pardeck tabulated the number of times each editorial board member was cited in social science literature during 1989. His results reinforced Lindsey's and Epstein's earlier research. The median citation frequencies for the editorial board members of psychology journals were as follows: Journal of Counseling Psychology (14.5); Journal of Applied Psychology (24.5); Journal of Abnormal Psychology (21); Journal of Educational Psychology (5); Journal of Personality and Social Psychology (83). The median citation frequencies for the social work journals were as follows: Social Service Review (8); Social Work (7); Journal of Social Work Education (1); Families in Society (4); Child Welfare (4). These differences were statistically significant between the journals of the two disciplines (Pardeck, 1992, p. 492). These findings are very similar to those described by Lindsey (1978a); in fact, of the 69 individuals on social work editorial boards in 1990, nearly one half were cited only three or fewer times in the *Social Sciences Citation Index* (1989). Pardeck concluded that many social work editorial board members did not achieve board membership on the basis of scholarly publishing in professional journals.

Pardeck, Chung, and Murphy (1995) reported findings on the scholarly productivity of editorial boards and guest reviewers for key social work journals. Scholarly productivity was defined by the number of citation counts and articles published by each board member and guest reviewer for the years 1987–1990. Many editorial board members appeared to have modest levels of scholarly productivity. Similar findings were reported for guest reviewers. For example, a substantial percentage of editorial board members and guest reviewers were cited only three times or less over the time period studied. Pardeck, Chung, and Murphy concluded that these findings were notable and had serious implications for the academic and professional credibility of social work.

Pardeck and Meinert (1999a,b) examined the scholarly distinction and achievements of the 8 editorial members and 47 consulting editors of the National Association of Social Work's (NASW) flagship journal, *Social Work*. Using the *Social Sciences Citation Index* and *Psychological Abstracts*, these researchers examined the number of articles published by *Social Work's* editorial board and the number of times these articles had been cited from 1990 to 1995. A pattern similar to those previously reported by Lindsey (1978a,b) and Pardeck (1992) emerged; 50 percent of the editorial board and 19.1 percent of the consulting editors did not have a single article listed in the abstracting resources reviewed over the 6-year time period of the study. Furthermore, the data reported that a significant percentage of the editorial board and consulting editors of *Social Work* did not appear to be active scholars in the area of journal publications during the first half of the 1990s; 50 percent of the editorial board and 23.4 percent of the consulting editors were cited only zero to three times over this six-year period. Findings from these studies contradicted the stated standards by NASW that "editorial board members must be NASW members in good standing and have a strong publishing background" (NASW, 2002). Pardeck and Meinert (1999a) cite a personal communication from a former NASW publications manager and managing editor of *Social Work* that the explicit policy of *Social Work* was to only appoint an individual to its editorial board if he or she was "an established scholar who has current experience and who has published articles in peer-reviewed journals in the field" (p. 89). Pardeck and Meinert (1999b) urged NASW to adopt a wider, more inclusive policy when selecting editorial board members, rather than continuing to rely on the informal network which appears to be currently in operation.

The researchers further expressed concern about the lack of scholarly attainments of these editorial board members who serve as gatekeepers for *Social Work* and other social work journals. They wondered whether less qualified judges were making important editorial recommendations. Pardeck and Meinert (1999b) concluded: "That *Social Work* is in serious violation of its own policy in this regard leads one to question whether high-quality articles are consistently being published" (p. 125).

On the other hand, one could understand that many of the editorial board members might have reached a particular stage of their professional careers that their emphases could be more on the administration of social work education programs, mentoring of new faculty and students, or engaging in community services than on academic or scholarly publication. Also, this study of publication record was exclusively on journal publications. These editorial members might have productive records of book publications or other creative and scholarly activities to their credit.

In a recent study, Kirk and Franke (1997) analyzed the reliability of editorial reviewers' manuscript evaluations. They analyzed the reviews of 54 articles that had been submitted to *Social Work Research* during 1994. The researcher examined the reviewers' consensus pertaining to the overall recommended disposition of each article (e.g., accept, reject and encourage major revisions, reject) and the reviewers' appraisals of nine stated aspects of the article's content (e.g., "The data support the conclusions"). Kirk and Franke (1997) found that the amount of agreement among the reviewers was low. These findings like earlier research on social work editorial boards question the competence of the reviewers.

Thyer and Polk (1997) in another study also report additional evidence for weak social work editorial boards. These researchers found that editorial board members of social work journals appear to publish less, and are cited less, than the editorial board members of journals from other disciplines. This finding mirrors earlier research (Pardeck, 1992) reporting low journal productivity among social work academics as a whole when compared to qualified psychology faculty. These findings like much of the earlier research reviewed in this chapter questions the commitment to research by social workers and the quality of social work editorial boards.

In a study on social work editorial boards, Lindsey (1999) confirmed Epstein's (1990a,b) concerns. Lindsey reported that not only were nonscientific and idiosyncratic standards used by social work editorial boards, but such standards were also employed by schools of social work when they select faculty for chaired professorships. He reports that a number of major research universities that have endowed professorships allow faculty to be appointed to these positions based on criteria other than scholarly merit. For example, one person was appointed to an endowed chair at a major university without one significant publication to the person's credit. Another prominent university with an endowed chair in social work appointed a person to the chair who had virtually never been cited in the social science literature. In contrast, at the same university, but in sociology, a distinguished scholar was appointed to an endowed chair in that department who had been cited in the literature extensively by others. Lindsey's findings offer another example of why the profession of social work lacks standing in the academic community (Meinert, Pardeck, and Krueger, 2000).

Again, in 2002, Pardeck explored the scholarly productivity of editors of selected social work and psychology journals. Pardeck employed a number of measures in his research, including how often editorial board members were cited by others and the number of articles they had published. Pardeck recognized that an editor's scholarly productivity may be defined by other factors. These include service activities to a field, the reputation of contributions to the field regardless of scholarly production levels, and presentations at conferences or contributions as an author or editor of books. Pardeck included the following leading social work journals in his research: *Families in Society*, *Social Service Review*, *Child Welfare*, *Journal of Social Work Education*, and *Social Work*. The journals included from the field of psychology were the *Journal of Counseling Psychology*, *Journal of Applied Psychology*, *Journal of Abnormal Psychology*, *Journal of Educational Psychology*, and *Journal of Personality and Social Psychology*. Earlier research on social work editorial boards by Lindsey (1978a,b) and Pardeck (1992) also analyzed the above journals.

In Pardeck's 2002 research, the measure he used to assess an editor's scholarly productivity was through the total number of articles published from January 1992 to June 2001. Mean scores from these totals were calculated for all editors from each discipline. The resource used to specify the number of articles published by each editor was from PsycINFO. PsycINFO abstracts every article from the major and minor social work journals. PsycINFO as compared to the Social Work Abstracts has greater validity for measuring scholarly productivity among social workers because of this wider coverage. Furthermore, many social workers also publish articles in allied fields not covered in the Social Work Abstracts (Green, Hutchison, and Sar, 1992).

The measure for determining an editor's scholarly "impact" was accomplished through the creation of the total number of citations

Table 5.1 Comparison of social work and psychology journal editors' average yearly publication and citation between 1992 and 2001

	Article	Citation
Social Work Editors		
Families in Society	2	0
Social Service Review	5	17.4
Child Welfare	0	6
Journal of Social Work Education	10	18.8
Social Work	0	9.6
	M=3.4	M=9.28
	SD=4.22	SD=8.92
Psychology Editors		
Journal of Counseling Psychology	21	53.5
Journal of Applied Psychology	26	83.6
Journal of Abnormal Psychology	20	18.7
Journal of Educational Psychology	40	131.4
Journal of Personality and Social Psychology	15	97
	M=24.4	M=76.82
	SD=9.5	SD=42.89

from the *Social Sciences Citation Index* for the years 1995–1999. Means from these totals were calculated for all editors from each discipline. A citation was counted only if the individual editor was the sole or first author of an article. Self-citations were not included in the citation counts.

In Table 5.1, it is clear that the average yearly article publication for the years 1992 through June 2001 for editors of the psychology journals are much greater than those reported for the social work journal editors. Table 5.1 also points out that the average number of citations for the years 1995 through 1999 for editors of psychology journals are greater than the average number of citations for social work editors.

Pardeck (2002) concluded that the findings should be viewed with the following limitations. Citation counts for the editors may be affected by the fact that the *Social Science Citation Index* covers a greater number of psychology than social work journals. Furthermore, Cheung (1990) reported that social work journals are not heavily cited by other disciplines. Even with these limitations, it is clear that editors of social work journals do not have a record of scholarly productivity and distinction as defined by this study, whereas editors of the selected psychology journals had clear records of scholarly achievement. These findings are similar to earlier research exploring the scholarly distinction and achievement of editorial board members of psychology and social work journals (Lindsey, 1978; Pardeck et al., 1991; Pardeck, 1992).

SUMMARY AND CONCLUSIONS

The field of social work since the 1970s has been aware of the lack of scholarly achievement by its practitioners and educators including editorial board members of social work journals. Furthermore, research by Pardeck, Chung, and Murphy (1995) reported that guest reviewers of social work journals also lack scholarly achievement. These findings inevitably impose a certain degree of suspicion on the fairness and quality of the articles published in these social work journals. They bolster the speculations that publication decisions may be based more in ideology than merit, which are established by rigorous peer expert reviews. Some outstanding papers may end up not finding the proper publication outlets that they deserve.

There also appears to be a lack of commitment to scholarship and scientific inquiry by social workers in general. As reported in this chapter, few social workers publish; this includes those who have a doctorate in social work. The lack of commitment has negatively affected the field of social work in its pursuit of the development, dissemination, and consumption of new knowledge. It may also contribute to the struggling status of social work among professionals and in university settings.

The field of social work graduates only a limited number of doctoral students each year. These students' training, interests, and responsibilities in knowledge development through scientific research are often not sufficiently promoted. The Masters of Social Work (MSW) is considered to be the terminal degree for practice. Although MSW education aims to prepare students to be practitioners as well as producers of knowledge, most often they end up more as consumers. MSW courses are watered down to be palatable for students who are unable to see research as an integral part of practice. Such diluted research content would not suffice in other disciplines. The lack of comparable research standards, which are found in other social sciences, means MSW graduates will continue to lack quality preparation in the area of research. Furthermore, few MSW programs offer, let alone require, a research thesis for students. This means that research generated by MSWs in the field and published in professional or academic journals is rare.

Given the fact that research is not a high priority in the field of social work, it should not be surprising to find that knowledge that has been generated by the field is not studied and disseminated to benefit the profession. Most knowledge used in social work, such as systems theory, is borrowed from other social sciences or professions. Social work needs to produce field-tested knowledge with clearly defined variables, intervention methods, and predictive outcomes. As long as social work lacks in the development of its own knowledge base, social work programs cannot offer students distinct and exclusive knowledge and skills that could achieve the professional mission. The field of social work needs to come up to speed with other disciplines in the area of knowledge production; if the field does not do so, it is questionable if social work will be a viable field in the twenty-first century. The noticeable increase in the number of social work journals and book publications in recent years may reflect the possibility that the field is on its way to claim its rightful place in the new century.

REFERENCES

Cheung, K. M. (1990). Interdisciplinary relationships between social work and other disciplines: A citation study. *Social Work Research and Abstracts*, 26, 23–29.

Epstein, W. (1990a). Confirmation response bias among social work journals. *Science, Technology, & Human Values*, 15, 9–38.

Epstein, W. (1990b). The obligation of intellectuals. *Science, Technology, & Human Values*, 15, 244–247.

Epstein, W. (1992). Thump therapy for social work journals. *Research on Social Work Practice*, 2(4), 525–528.

Fraser, M. W., Taylor, M. J., Jackson, R., & O'Jack, J. (1991). Social work and science: Many ways of knowing? *Social Work Research Abstracts*, 27, 5–15.

Green, R., Hutchison, E., & Sar, B. (1992). Evaluating scholarly performance: the productivity of graduates of social work doctoral programs. *Social Service Review*, 66, 441–446.

Kirk, S. A. & Franke, T. M. (1997). Agreeing to disagree: A study of the reliability of manuscript reviews. *Social Work Research*, 21, 121–126.

Lindsey, D. (1976). Distinction, achievement, and editorial board membership. *American Psychologist*, 31, 799–804.

Lindsey, D. (1977a). Participation and influence in publication review proceedings: A reply. *American Psychologist*, 32, 579–586.

Lindsey, D. (1977b). The processing of self-criticism by social work journals. *American Psychologist*, 32, 1110–1115.

Lindsey, D. (1978a). *The scientific publication system in social science: A study of the operation of leading professional journals in psychology, sociology, and social work*. San Francisco: Jossey-Bass.

Lindsey, D. (1978b). The operations of professional journals in social work. *Journal of Sociology and Social Welfare*, 5, 273–298.

Lindsey, D. (1999). Ensuring standards in social work research. *Research on Social Work Practice*, 9, 115–120.

Mahoney M. (1977). Publication prejudices: An experimental study of confirmatory bias in the peer review system. *Cognitive Therapy and Research*, 1(2), 161–175.

Meinert, R., Pardeck, J. T., & Kreuger, L. (2000). *Social work: Seeking Relevancy in the Twenty-First Century*. Binghamton, NY: The Haworth Press.

Pardeck, J. T. (1992). Are social work journal editorial boards competent? Some disquieting data with implications for research on social work practice. *Research on Social Work Practice*, 2, 487–496.

Pardeck, J. T. (2002). Scholarly productivity of editors of social work and psychology journals. *Psychological Reports*, 90, 1051–1054.

Pardeck, J. T., Arndt, B. J., Light, D. B., Mosley, G. F., Thomas, S. D., Werner, M. A., & Wilson, K. E. (1991). Distinction and achievement levels of editorial board members of psychology and social work journals. *Psychological Reports*, 68, 523–527.

Pardeck, J. T., Chung, W., & Murphy, J. (1995). *Research on Social Work Practice*, 5, 223–234.

Pardeck, J. T. & Meinert, R. (1999a). Scholarly achievements of the Social Work editorial board and consulting editors: A commentary. *Research on Social Work Practice*, 9, 86–91.

Pardeck, J. T. & Meinert, R. (1999b). Improving the scholarly quality of Social Work's editorial board and consulting editors: A professional obligation. *Research on Social Work Practice*, 9, 121–127.

Peters, D. & Ceci, S. (1982). Peer review practices of psychological journals: The fate of published articles submitted again. *Behavioral and Brain Sciences*, 5(2), 187–195.

Thyer, B. A. & Polk, G. (1997). Social work and psychology professors' scholarly productivity: A controlled comparison of cited journal articles. *Journal of Applied Social Sciences*, 21, 105–110.

Chapter 6

Advancing the Profession of Social Work in the Twenty-first Century

Significant changes in a number of critical areas are important for the further improvement of the profession of social work. These include improving the quality of social work journals, committing to knowledge development, retuning and rethinking social work education, and promoting sound and accountable social work practice. A final area of concern, which is essential to all these discussions, is the effective application of critical thinking. These areas of concern with strategies for improvement are presented in Table 6.1 below.

Table 6.1 Area of concern with recommended strategies for improvement

Area of Concern	Strategies to Improve
Social Work Journals	○ Appoint editorial boards and editors with scholarly records
Knowledge Development	○ Create a knowledge base unique to social work
Professional Education	○ Greater emphasis on scientific approach to practice in both BSW and MSW curricula
	○ Expansion of Doctoral Social Work Programs
Social Work Practice	○ Increase the use of practice models that are grounded in sound and rigorous social and scientific knowledge
Critical Thinking	○ Promote open and constructive criticism among social workers when analyzing the effectiveness of social work practice and social work education

SOCIAL WORK JOURNALS

It is clear from research over the past 30 years that social work journals often lack a commitment to scholarship. As noted in this work, many social work editorial boards, guest reviewers, and even editors do not have solid records of scholarly productivity. Given this fact, one must speculate on how persons are chosen to review articles for publication in social work journals. It would appear reasonable to conclude that choices for board assignment are often not the result of the reviewers' record of scholarship. As noted in the previous chapter on editorial boards, related disciplines such as psychology or sociology that appoint reviewers based on scholarly productivity are defined by solid records of publication. What is particularly unfortunate when editorial boards are appointed on criteria that do not include a record of scholarship is they are the very people who make the decision about what is published in a journal. Refereed journals are the engines and the fountains for the development of theory, intervention techniques, and knowledge for the profession. The quality of journal publication has direct effects on the quality of services that clients receive. Thirty years of research illustrating the limitations of social work journals needs to be taken more seriously by those operating social work journals; if anything, not doing so would appear to be unethical.

It has also been noted by Stoesz (1997) that social work journals often have lumbering publication procedures that retard the development of new knowledge. Many social work journals do not publish articles until months or years after acceptance. The review period of the article may take 4 to 6 months. By the time the article is published through such a process, the information is dated.

Thyer (2004) cites an extreme example of an October 2003 publication in *Social Work* by Cunningham (2003) that took over 4 years from its initial submission to the date it was published. Thyer surveyed authors who published in 21 major social work journals in 2000 and found that it "took, on average, over 19 months to receive an initial decision letter from *Social Work*, and a further 12 months for the article to see print" (Thyer, 2004, p. 362). He argues that this kind of delay also contributes to the low impact score of social work journals by the Social Sciences Citation Index (SSCI). "The SSCI impact score measures how often the typical article in a specific journal is cited for that year" (p. 361). Simplistically speaking, an article published in a journal with an impact score of 2 is on an average two times more likely to be cited as compared to a similar article published in a journal with a score of 1. "In 2002 no social work disciplinary journal's impact factor appeared to exceed 1.0" (p. 362), but the impact factor "for the *American Psychologist* was a whopping 5.9" (p. 362). Thyer points out that the time-sensitive nature and the manner in which the SSCI impact factor is being calculated indicates that it "can be seen to be a poor comparative measure of journal quality" (pp. 362–363). In spite of the score's limitations, Thyer suggests that social work academics should still pay attention to the impact score.

This type of lengthy delay prevents social workers from learning about the latest research findings in a timely manner. Stoesz (1997) also concludes that editors often lack competence in operating journals and the necessary expertise to judge the scientific merit of an article. Discussions in previous chapters echo Stoesz's position.

One of the authors of this book (Pardeck) suggests a radical strategy for reforming appointments to an editorial board: the role of guest reviewer or editor. Treat the opportunity to review articles the same way as one applies for an academic position. Each year, editors of social work journals might simply have various social workers with different areas of expertise apply to the journal through a selection process that resembles job applications. The potential reviewers must clearly demonstrate that they have a record of publications in that area and that they have the skills to make an objective decision about an article's academic and professional merit. Such a process would reduce the political aspect of reviewer assignment and would appear to lead to the publication of articles that are meritorious. It is a noteworthy strategy but its feasibility and practicality remain to be seen.

A relatively less complicated process may just be upholding the standard of a record of scholarly productivity as a key requirement for such editorial board appointments. Serving on an editorial board of a professional journal should be a prestigious achievement that signifies the recognition of one's expertise in the profession. In addition to established scholarship records, editorial boards should also consider the potential board member's additional area of expertise, years of practice experience, and other diversity factors. To ensure journal publications have relevance to direct practice and to bridge the gaps between the academic world and the practice world, certain board member openings should be reserved for MSW or doctoral-level practitioners. For those same reasons, practitioners should be strongly encouraged and supported to submit articles for publication considerations.

Collaborative practice research between academics and practitioners is a great avenue to develop literature that is both based in theory and grounded in practice. This kind of arrangement will ensure first and foremost the scholarly standards of the board. It strives to gain balanced perspectives and respect for diversity. It provides mentoring opportunities as well as encourages participation and cooperation in practice-relevant scholarly activities by both the social work practitioners and educators. It could develop an editorial board that is not an exclusive club for the "elites" or become a "good-ole-boy" network; but a diverse, representative, and scholarly board. These approaches are not new strategies; many journals have adopted such approaches. The concern is how we could promote such approaches to more of the social work journals.

Committees or administrators who are responsible for making decisions about appointment, retention, tenure, and promotion to social work positions may also be able to improve the quality of social work journals. They could place a stronger emphasis on encouraging faculty to publish in journals that have the proven rigor and quality of academic and scientific inquiry. It would seem that such an emphasis from the university administrators would gradually encourage social work faculty and social work journals to give greater commitment to the quality of scholarship and knowledge development. Until strategies such as these are employed, the quality of scholarship will continue to suffer and just as importantly the status of social work in higher education will continue to have limited standing.

SOCIAL WORK KNOWLEDGE BASE

A solid knowledge base is one of the critical components for determining if a profession is truly that. The interdependent and interrelated nature of knowledge dictates the beneficial exchange and fusion of knowledge across professions and disciplines. Social work knowledge could come from many sources including traditions, practice wisdom and clinical experiences, scientific studies, as well as knowledge borrowed from many disciplines such as sociology, psychiatry, psychology, anthropology, economics, and mathematics. Medical science also borrows knowledge from disciplines such as biology, chemistry, pharmacology, physics, engineering, economics, and sociology. It is through the medical scientists' constant efforts in integrating borrowed knowledge with their own practice and clinical experience and putting them to rigorous scientific study that medical science is able to advance its own exclusive and solid knowledge base and professional status. The development of an integrated knowledge base and its associated skills unique to social work is probably one of the most pressing issues for the profession in the twenty-first century.

The postmodern view dominating social work has advanced the profession in certain manners. However, it also fails to promote a pro-scientific orientation in the field that makes it difficult for developing empirically based practice. It was noted that much of the knowledge used by social workers to guide their practice is not only borrowed from other disciplines but also that what is borrowed often does not necessarily have a scientific grounding. Until social workers become more attuned to thinking and using methods based in scientific inquiry and evidence, the quality of services offered by practitioners will be suspect.

Practice experience is one of the most important modalities for developing a new knowledge base in the field of social work. Experience however often has many limitations because it involves the subjective interpretation of the practitioner concerning what works or does not work in practice. If practice wisdom and experience are the strength of the profession, then social work should build upon its strengths. Through scientific methodology and critical analysis, the social work profession could further validate these experiences and prove their effectiveness and utility in serving clients' needs. The application of scientific approach therefore is key to the development of proven knowledge for the profession.

Current CSWE requires a minimal two years of practice experience as a prerequisite to teach practice courses. This requirement should also be coupled with the additional emphasis on teaching scientific foundation and critical thinking for social work practice, practice research, and theory development. Hopefully, with the increased focus and interest in the application of scientific approach to practice, the social work profession could more rapidly build its own knowledge base that is scientifically sound and is grounded in practice experience.

It is critical that practitioners publish their findings on scientific-based practice in social work journals. Journals are critical to the dissemination of new knowledge. It would appear to be a professional obligation for social work practitioners to publish their theory, experience, and study findings on various practice techniques used so others might also use them.

Systems theory and ecological perspective offer social workers frameworks to understand the dynamics between individuals and their environments. They are however limited in providing guidelines for practice and lack scientific grounding. To build upon these current prevalent theoretical orientations, social workers may consider models such as the ecosystem-oriented assessment-intervention approach, a model that incorporates the ecosystem perspectives while providing steps of intervention that are practical and workable in practice settings (Pardeck,

1996). Such an approach should be scientifically based and utilize evidence from ongoing assessment and evaluation of interventions by tools such as validated clinical instruments. By using such an approach, the field will push itself to be more evidence based; this will ultimately benefit clients. Currently, there are many practice models that are empirically based, for example, evidence-based practice (Corcoran, 2003; Gibbs, 2003; Cournoyer, 2004), solution-focused therapy (De Jong and Berg, 2002), and task-centered approach (Reid and Epstein, 1972; Reid, 1992).

Social work education must play a crucial role in the development of new knowledge for the profession. A core tradition of the university is to develop new knowledge in various fields of study; social work programs must play this critical role in the university.

PROFESSIONAL SOCIAL WORK EDUCATION

Social work education has many challenges. These include the ongoing refinement in the development and implementation of CSWE accreditation standards, the lack of doctoral-level educated faculty who also have sufficient practice experience, and faculty members who may not have strong interests in scholarship and scientific inquiry.

The work by Gambrill (1997, pp. 318–320) highlights many of the limitations of social work education. The following synopsis reflects what Gambrill views as problems and issues related to teaching effectiveness in social work education:

1. Social work education is often indoctrination rather than education. Many social work faculties appear to be the authority who certifies what is important or not important in terms of the educational process. They do not like being challenged and do not encourage students to do critical thinking.
2. Social work educators have a tendency to actively promote ignorance. Students are not encouraged to read arguments outside the field or to critique the popular viewpoints in the field.
3. Social work faculty may not pay enough attention to the results of educational research. Educational methods that work and scientific findings about teaching effectiveness are not fully utilized to improve teaching effectiveness.
4. Similarly, social work faculty do not aggressively assess competencies and outcomes of the educational process. This means that faculty members may not know if their teaching has been effective and achieves the desirable outcomes.

5. Social work faculty sometime promote fads and rituals. New ideas that are untested may be presented in the classroom and taught to students as being effective techniques for practice.

Much of the criticism noted above by Gambrill is consistent with the empirical findings reported in the previous chapter on social work education. Many social work curricula do not always sufficiently prepare students to carry out their professional responsibilities; students appear not to grow in self-awareness and social workers who are licensed without being exposed to social work education appear to acquire social work skills, knowledge, and values at the same levels as those who graduate from social work programs. These are serious issues that should be of concern for the field in the twenty-first century.

One of the challenges for social work education is the insufficient number of graduate faculty members who have adequate practice experience as well as doctoral-level preparation for research and knowledge development. This situation has been improved in recent years by the increased emphasis on having a doctoral degree for hiring or for retention. Few fields of study in the university setting are allowed to hire faculty without doctorates.

It should be noted that many of these non-doctoral faculty members are outstanding teachers and mentors to their fellow doctoral faculty and students. Their educational backgrounds however may not have prepared them to engage in higher-level research activities. This situation still does not preclude them from having advanced expertise in research. Many have developed such knowledge and proficiency through practice and specialized training. Nevertheless, it is more likely that research for scholarship is not a main focus of their academic assignments. Conversely, it is also noted that many doctoral-level social work faculty have limited appreciation and skills for research and scientific inquiry. A doctoral degree may not guarantee commitment to research and scholarly productivity. It only assumes that doctoral-level faculty members are prepared and may be more likely to engage in such activities. Lack of a doctoral degree does not preclude one from becoming a researcher and productive scholar.

One solution to this problem is to produce more doctoral-level social work graduates who are well trained in research and practice evaluation. The CSWE could require that all teachers and administrators in social work programs must have a MSW and a doctorate in social work or closely related fields. As noted earlier in this chapter, higher level university administrators also need to play a more active role in promoting scholarship through the tenure and hiring process. If these changes do not occur, social work education will remain stuck in neutral for years to come.

Finally, what should be noted with the suggestions above is that they simply require social work programs to behave as other academic programs do in the academy. A number of social worker programs have done that, but there is little or no excuse to do otherwise.

SOCIAL WORK PRACTICE

The critical analysis of social work practice suggests that the methods used by social workers in practice lack adequate scientific support. Furthermore, systems theory and the ecological perspective, currently the core foundation theories for social work practice, are not sufficient to guide effective practice. It is a necessity for social work in the twenty-first century to further developing focus on methods of intervention and theories generated and supported by scientific processes.

Chapter 2 presents an overview of the major intervention methods in social work practice. Many empirically based methods have been proposed by social work practitioners and educators. Clinical therapeutic approaches that employ clinical instruments were presented and could be incorporated for effective social work practice. A possible alternative model for social work practice, the ecosystem-oriented assessment-intervention approach was suggested by one of the authors (Pardeck) as an example. It may be a starting point for developing intervention approaches that are guided by systematically collected evidence.

Each step of the ecosystem-oriented assessment-intervention approach allows the practitioner to operationalize the ecological perspective based interventions so that they can be assessed and evaluated in terms of their effectiveness. It also calls for the use of clinical instruments. Even though the ecosystem-oriented assessment-intervention approach continues to need further development, it provides a draft framework for a professional-scientist model of social work.

CRITICAL THINKING

Gambrill (1997) argues that social workers must shift from being believers to being questioners. In other words, social workers need to do more critical thinking about what they teach in the classroom and the methods they use during service delivery. Only through such a process will social work as a field move to a more fully professional status like other helping professions. Critical thinking is defined as (Mayer and Goodchild, 1990):

An active, systematic process of understanding and evaluating arguments. An argument provides an assertion about the properties of some object or the relationship between two or more objects and evidence to support or refute the assertion. Critical thinkers acknowledge that there is no single correct way to understand and evaluate arguments and that all attempts are not necessarily successful (p. 4).

More often than not, discussions in social work are within frameworks rather than about them (Popper, 1994). An example might be to assume that the basic principles guiding systems theory are correct and not to challenge these principles because they are assumed to be correct. In another example, pronouncements are made by social work educators in the classroom without accompanying argument or evidence. Experiences of effective social work practice need to be validated and organized by critical analysis and refinement. Only through this process, these valuable experiences could be developed into practice knowledge and then properly disseminated and utilized.

Popper (1992) believes that only through critical thinking will social workers find solutions to problems about classroom or practice effectiveness; this process allows one to learn more about problems and the kind of corrective actions that need to be taken to solve problems that impact teaching or service delivery. He highlights the basis of rational discussion, a critical component that could further the process of critical thinking. The following summarizes the major components for rational discussion as proposed by Popper (1992, p. 199):

1. The principle of fallibility: This means I may be wrong and perhaps your are right too. But we both might be wrong.
2. The principle of rational discussion: When using this kind of discussion, we attempt to be as impersonal as possible, to weigh up our reasons for and against a theory–a theory that is definite and criticizable.
3. The principle of approximation to the truth: This means we can nearly always come closer to the truth in a discussion that avoids personal attacks on others. This can help us achieve a better understanding even in those areas where we do not reach an agreement.

Popper (1994) further argues that truth allows us to move toward statements of fact. That is, valuing truth over prejudice and ignorance entails critical thinking that involves measurement and supported conclusions. If a social worker states, "I have helped this client," this claim should correspond with the evidence. Only through evaluation of practice effectiveness can a social worker make sound conclusions about whether an intervention plan is working or not. Popper (1994) emphasizes that unexamined claims about effectiveness reflect a kind of ignorance that is at odds with compassion for others. Popper (1992) concludes:

It is important never to forget our ignorance. We should never pretend to know anything, and we should never use big words. What I call the cardinal sin... is simply talking hot air, professing a wisdom we do not possess (p. 86).

Gambrill (1997) echoes a similar sentiment that we have an obligation never to pose as a prophet, even though it is hard for us to resist soothsayers who often rely on tradition, common sense, anecdotal experience, and practice experience as the basis for supporting truth.

Another suggested strategy that social workers may also wish to consider is to use more critical thinking in education and practice. Social workers could conduct various critical analyses focusing on the values, knowledge, and skills that guide the field of social work. This kind of inquiry will help social workers to become more responsive and effective in meeting clients' needs. Lipman (1991) refers to this process as an approach for achieving a community of inquiry, a process that involves the following examples of critical thinking:

- Focusing on critical discussion and measurement of claims rather than on justifying them.
- Developing awareness that we are all equal in our ignorance.
- The valuing of truth over ignorance.
- An appreciation for errors and mistakes that should be viewed as learning opportunities.
- The discarding of authority as a basis to knowledge.
- The position that knowledge is always tentative.
- The valuing of clashing points of view as invaluable for discovering truth.

The above ideas enhance social workers' abilities in differentiating facts from fiction and identifying effective problem-solving approaches.

Finally, Gambrill (1997) argues that educational research can help move the field of social work forward. Gambrill supports the position that social workers should use teaching methods that are most likely to enable students to acquire knowledge and skills that work in practice. Furthermore, social work practice should employ competent approaches that have proven to be effective. Professional organizations such as the National Association of Social Workers (NASW) and Council on Social Work Education (CSWE) have major responsibilities in moving social workers toward being inquirers and not simply believers.

CONCLUSIONS AND IMPLICATIONS

In this chapter, five areas of concern for improving social work were discussed. These include the quality of social work journals, knowledge development, professional education, social work practice and critical thinking. It has been emphasized in this book that the field of social work must place greater emphasis on using scientific approaches in practice. It is critical for social work faculty to teach scientific and evidence-based interventions and to teach students how to measure practice outcomes. A number of strategies were suggested that could help to achieve this goal.

Another important concern that affects knowledge development for the field is that social work education and social work practice need to place greater importance on scholarly productivity. Coinciding with the increase of publishers with a greater interest in publishing social work texts, an increasing number of social workers and educators are also becoming serious and active in publications. They should be supported and commended for their scholarly interest. Meanwhile, the quality of scholarship would also be promoted by improving the criteria and process for appointment of editorial boards, guest reviewers, and editors.

Finally, building on the achievements of the current education programs, social work professional training can be further refined and improved in various dimensions. These include hiring more doctoral-level faculty trained in research and evaluation with sufficient practice experience and placing greater emphasis on scholarship in social work education. In fact, one might argue that the most pressing need to improve the field of social work in the twenty-first century may begin in the academy.

REFERENCES

Corcoran, J. (2003). *Clinical applications of evidence-based family interventions*. New York: Oxford Press.
Cournoyer, B. (2004). *The evidence-based social work skills book*. Boston, MA: Pearson.

Cunningham, M. (2003). Impact of trauma work on social work clinicians: Empirical findings. *Social Work*, 48, 451–459.

De Jong, P. & Berg, I. K. (2002). *Interviewing for solutions* (2nd ed.). Pacific Grove, CA: Wadsworth.

Gambrill, E. (1997). Social work education: Current concerns and possible futures. In M. Reisch & E. Gambrill (Eds.), *Social work in the 21st century* (317–327). Thousand Oaks, CA: Sage.

Gibbs, L. (2003). *Evidence-based practice for the helping professionals: A practical guide with integrated multimedia*. Pacific Grove, CA: Brooks/Cole.

Lipman, M. (1991). *Thinking in education*. Cambridge: Cambridge University Press.

Mayer, R. & Goodchild, F. (1990). *The critical thinker*. New York: Wm. C. Brown.

Pardeck, J. T. (1996). *Social work practice: An ecological approach*. Westport, CT: Auburn House.

Popper, K. (1992). *In search of a better world: Lectures and essays from thirty years*. New York: Routledge.

Popper, K. (1994). *The myth of the framework: In defense of science and rationality*. London: Routledge.

Reid, W. (1992). *Task strategies: An empirical approach to clinical social work*. New York: Columbia University Press.

Reid, W. & Epstein, L. (1972). *Task-centered practice*. New York: Columbia University Press.

Stoesz, D. (1997). The end of social work. In M. Reisch & E. Gambrill (Eds.), *Social work in the 21st century*. (368–375). Thousand Oaks, CA: Sage.

Thyer, B. (2004). Letter to the editor: Evaluating social work journal publication system. *Journal of Social Work Education*, 40(2), 361–363.

Index

About the Authors

JOHN T. PARDECK was Professor Emeritus in the School of Social Work at Southwest Missouri State University. He authored *Social Work After the Americans with Disabilities Act: New Challenges and Opportunities for Social Services Professionals* (Auburn House, 1998), and was a guiding force behind the *Journal of Social Work In Disability & Rehabilitation*, where he served as editor until his death in 2004.

FRANCIS YUEN is Professor in the Division of Social Work, California State University, Sacramento.